GUIDE TO AESTHETICS

GUIDE TO AESTHETICS

(*Breviario di estetica*)

BENEDETTO CROCE

Translated, with
Introduction and notes, by
PATRICK ROMANELL

Hackett Publishing Company, Inc.
Indianapolis/Cambridge

Benedetto Croce: 1866–1952
Breviario di estetica was originally published in 1913.

00   99   98   2   3   4   5   6   7

For further information, please address

Hackett Publishing Company, Inc.
P.O. Box 44937
Indianapolis, Indiana 46244–0937

Cover design by Listenberger Design & Associates

Library of Congress Cataloging-in-Publication Data

Croce, Benedetto, 1866–1952.
    [Breviario di estetica. English]
    Guide to aesthetics = Breviario di estetica/Benedetto Croce:
translated, with introduction and notes, by Patrick Romanell.
        p.   cm.
    Previously published: Indianapolis, IN: Bobbs-Merrill Co., c1965.
    Includes bibliographical references.
    ISBN 0-87220-305-0 (alk. paper).
    ISBN 0-87220-304-2 (pbk.: alk. paper)
    1. Aesthetics, Italian—20th century.   I. Romanell, Patrick, 1912–
    II. Title.
B3614.C73B7413   1995
111′.85—dc20   94-43408
                                                      CIP

CONTENTS

Introduction

Benedetto Croce's *Guide to Aesthetics,* a new translation of his *Breviario di estetica* which is appearing here for the first time, is the work of the only Italian philosopher in the twentieth century to have achieved international recognition as well as national fame. Born of a wealthy upper middle-class family on February 25, 1866, in Pescasseroli, Aquila (in the Abruzzi region of central Italy bordering on the Adriatic), Croce spent most of his versatile life as philosopher, scholar, historian, statesman, critic, editor, and publicist, in the ancient and loquacious Mediterranean city of Naples, where he died at the age of eighty-six on November 20, 1952.[1] Prolific and polemical writer[2] that he was, Croce has meant different things to different people, and even to the same people at different times.

By way of illustration, many of us outside Italy proudly remember Croce as that brave Abruzzian spirit who, endowed with a sharp tongue and a biting pen, dared almost single-handedly to oppose Fascism at its roots, defending against all odds the cause of truth, human dignity, and liberty. On the other hand, Giuseppe Prezzolini, an observer of Italian culture much closer to the scene, not only remembers him with a lament, as "the great unheeded man of Italy," but remains puzzled as to "why this powerful thinker—the most outstanding Italian since 1900, whose widespread influence is recognizable even in the minds of his opponents—did not exert a greater influence

---

[1] For biographical details on Croce, see Benedetto Croce, *An Autobiography,* trans. R. G. Collingwood (Oxford: Clarendon Press, 1927), and Cecil J. S. Sprigge, *Benedetto Croce: Man and Thinker* (New Haven: Yale University Press, 1952).

[2] For the complete bibliography of Croce's writings, see Fausto Nicolini, *L' "editio ne varietur" delle opere di B. Croce,* V (Naples: Biblioteca del "Bollettino" dell'Archivio Storico del Banco di Napoli, 1960).

on his own people at critical moments of their history."[3] An illustrious but tragic example of an individual who changed his mind about Croce (for obvious political reasons) is Giovanni Gentile (1875–1944), Croce's one-time personal friend and intellectual collaborator, who holds both the honor of having been the most rigorous neo-Hegelian in the entire history of Western philosophy and the dishonor of having been the official philosopher of Fascism in Italy.[4] Now, whatever Croce may have meant to this or that person or group inside or outside Italy, I am personally of the opinion that, in the long run, he will be remembered primarily for his insights into the field of aesthetics. Before seeing, however, the specific form that these insights take in his system of thought, it would be well to take up first his general insight into the theoretical significance of the aesthetic field itself.

I. THE PRIMACY OF AESTHETICS IN CROCE'S THOUGHT

That Italy enjoys an enviable place in the world of art is common knowledge, but what is little known is that the philosophy of art made its first appearance as an autonomous discipline in that historic land of Western culture, rather than, as frequently claimed, in Germany. Croce, who is very well-versed in the history of aesthetics in the West, has made this historical fact quite clear.

According to his findings on the subject, there is no doubt that Alexander Baumgarten (1714–1762) of Germany was actually the first person to coin the term *Aesthetica* and to use it to connote a "special science";[5] the term appeared initially in his doctoral dissertation (written in Latin) on the nature of

[3] Giuseppe Prezzolini, "Croce, Benedetto" in *Columbia Dictionary of Modern European Literature,* ed. Horatio Smith (New York: Columbia University Press, 1947), p. 180.

[4] For the bitter polemic between Croce and Gentile, see Patrick Romanell, *Croce versus Gentile: A Dialogue on Contemporary Italian Philosophy* (New York: S. F. Vanni, 1946).

[5] Croce, *Estetica come scienza dell'espressione e linguistica generale,* 6th ed. (Bari: Laterza, 1928), p. 234.

poetry, published in 1735 (reprinted by Croce in 1900). This disciple of Christian Wolff, however, was so steeped in the tradition of Leibnizian rationalism that he failed to use his own new term in the "modern" sense. Actually, he used the term "aesthetics" to signify a science subordinate to logic, that is, a special science dealing with the "inferior knowledge" of the senses, the optimum form of which, in his view, constitutes beauty itself. In other words, he did not use the term properly, that is, to mean a science enjoying its own autonomy. Therefore, the real "father" of aesthetics is not Baumgarten. Who, then, is he?

For Croce, "the first discoverer of aesthetic science"[6] as such is the "revolutionary" Neapolitan philosopher Giambattista Vico (1668–1744), the great Italian opponent of Cartesianism who was culturally born way ahead of his age, and whose intellectual originality is just now beginning to be appreciated outside Italy. As Vico in his *New Science* (1725) is the first to discover the Promised Land of Aesthetics, so Croce is the last to explore its exact boundaries. But we are getting ahead of our story, and we shall have to wait until later to see the significance of Croce's relation to Vico.

Meanwhile, I believe that the greatest over-all contribution of Croce to philosophy in general and to philosophy of art in particular lies in that he, more deliberately and more successfully than anyone else in the past, has made the field itself of aesthetics philosophically respectable, as a result of his having made an excellent case for its primacy in the understanding of human life. Until the time of his vigorous crusade to recover art's own legitimate rights, aesthetics had, as a general rule, only a second- or third-class citizenship in the realm of philosophy. This pathetic state of affairs was essentially brought about, according to our author, by a methodological "bias" implicit or explicit in Western philosophy since antiquity. This bias rests on the dubious assumption that there is a hierarchy of knowledge, and that knowledge obtained via intuition is necessarily "inferior" to knowledge obtained via intellect. Given this

6 *Ibid.,* p. 242.

unfounded assumption in the first place, no wonder that aesthetics as the philosophy of art, concerned as it is with man's
power of creative imagination, became methodologically suspect and was relegated to a subordinate place in the scheme of
things. And no wonder, as we are about to see, that the early
Croce around the turn of the century took upon himself the
important task of keeping theory of art free of every "hodgepodge,"[7] "intellectualistic" and otherwise.

Before proceeding to the general cultural situation out of
which Croce's own theory of art was to develop as a protest
against the ruling school of thought in the last third of the nineteenth century, it behooves us not to misunderstand his insistence on the primacy of aesthetics. When Croce insists on its
philosophic import, he does not mean that the ways of art are
"superior," say, to the ways of logic. All he means is that the subject matter of aesthetics is neither inferior nor superior to the
subject matter of logic, but, on the contrary, just as valuable,
philosophically. In this connection, he argues convincingly as
follows: "An inadequate Aesthetic must of necessity carry with it
an inadequate Logic."[8] For if we start from a false conception of
art, we cannot finish with a true conception of reasoning, since
the proper distinction between the two would be, of course,
missing. Besides, "all the controversies" about the "superiority"
of one form of human activity over another turn out to be
"foolish," because all of them have need of each other anyway.[9]
Incidentally, this is at bottom what the Crocian doctrine of the
"circularity" of the spirit is all about, despite the forbidding
language in which it is unfortunately couched.

II. CROCE'S REVOLT AGAINST POSITIVISM

At the time that Croce was a young man, the school of philosophy prevailing in his cultural milieu was Positivism. Its
foreign master most in vogue then in Italy was the English evo-

[7] *Ibid.*, p. 236.
[8] *Ibid.*, p. 47.
[9] Croce, *Filosofia, Poesia, Storia* (Milan: Ricciardi, 1951), p. 76.

lutionist Herbert Spencer, and its leading Italian spokesmen were Roberto Ardigò in philosophy and Cesare Lombroso in sociology. Croce revolted against their *scientificismo* ("scientism") with alacrity. His revolt is recorded in his first philosophical essays, *Primi saggi,* the earliest of which were written in 1893 and 1894. In retrospect, the author reports that these essays on aesthetics and historiography record the moment when "the hard ice of positivism was beginning to melt"[10] in Italy and elsewhere. The essays are certainly worth reading for the light they throw on the making of Croce's mind, as well as on the unmaking of the nineteenth-century varieties of positivism.

In order to understand the early Croce's violent reaction against positivism and Spencer, whose aesthetic ideas are cavalierly dismissed as "absolutely puerile," it must be remembered that positivists and evolutionists in general at the time looked at art in crude hedonistic and utilitarian terms, some reducing the beautiful "to a type of pleasure," some (like Spencer himself), to play.[11] Others even went so far as to take poetry, art, and beauty all the way back to the "sexual instinct or animal prehistory," describing them as "a sort of lust purified and pacified."[12] As examples of the physiological variety of positivistic aesthetics, Croce quotes Paolo Mantegazza, who sought to "put the Beautiful on the anatomy table and make an autopsy of it," and Dr. Mario Pilo, who analyzed the beautiful in terms of a "visceral aesthetic sense."[13] Echoes of the early Croce's rebellion against the hedonistic and materialistic "hodgepodge"

---

[10] Croce, *Primi saggi* (Bari: Laterza, 1919), p. viii.

[11] *Ibid.,* pp. 8–9. For the sake of the record, it should be added that subsequently, under a new set of circumstances which reflect the eventual victory of the New Idealism in Italy, Croce toned down considerably his attitude against positivism. Cf. *A History of Italy, 1871–1915,* trans. Cecilia M. Ady (Oxford: Clarendon Press, 1929), where he refers to "the reaction against positivism" (p. 240) in Italy at the dawn of the century and admits that the positivistic movement was, after all, an improvement over "certain hasty conclusions and false analogies of which the idealist philosophy of the preceding generation has been guilty" (p. 141).

[12] *Ibid.,* pp. ix–x.

[13] *Ibid.,* p. 162.

in aesthetics, popular during the heyday of positivism, can be heard in the opening of his mature work that is translated here, the *Breviario,* written in 1912 and published the following year.

Croce in 1894 wrote a challenging essay "On the Present Conditions of Literary Studies in Italy and Their Deficiency." He finds that they suffered from three chief defects. One is that they were narrow in scope, being "too restricted to Italian literary history alone."[14] Urging Italian literary scholars to adopt the wise policy of their German counterparts, Croce makes a plea for the intensive study of foreign literatures in Italy. The second defect has to do with the poor quality of the literary studies in question. Croce here complains that their learned authors had become so engrossed in "little things" and "minutiae"[15] that they had lost sight of the forest for the trees. Lastly, he submits, the third and "greatest defect" of the literary studies in Italy at the time stems from their "neglect of theoretical problems." This neglect was caused partly, he explains, by a "legitimate reaction against the empty generalizing in fashion at one time," partly to that "gay philosophy which is positivism," and partly to the ensuing "ignorance."[16]

Moreover, the positivistic outlook on things prevalent in Croce's midst during his formative years was reflected not only in literary history and criticism, but also in the current novels, short stories, dramas, and, with the single exception of the great Italian poet Giosuè Carducci, in the poetry of the period. In fact, the foreign writer most imitated and emulated at that time in Italy, especially by the devotees of *verismo* ("verism," the Italian term for "naturalism" in literature), was the French novelist Émile Zola, who, having come under the acknowledged influence of the great French pioneer in experimental medicine Claude Bernard, argued from analogy and theorized about the "experimental novel." Now, given this general cultural atmosphere surrounding Croce's early life—which stifled a sensitive

14 *Ibid.,* p. 156.
15 *Ibid.,* pp. 157–158.
16 *Ibid.,* p. 158.

soul like his, spelling as it did for him "scientific fanaticism" and the "cult" of *mere* "facts"—is it any surprise that our fighting philosopher at fiery Naples decided in 1902 to launch a campaign on behalf of the "reawakening and modernization of philosophy"?[17] The outcome of this decision was the appearance of a new journal, *La Critica,* which was edited for over forty years (1903–1944) as virtually a one-man operation bringing to its editor all sorts of national and international honors and heartaches.

III. SOURCES OF CROCE'S AESTHETIC THOUGHT

Croce's aesthetics, which is integral to his "Philosophy of Spirit," constituting as it does the first part of an elaborate four-part neo-idealistic system of philosophy, is a complex product composed of many strands of thought and so defies exact classification. Nevertheless, historically speaking, his thesis in aesthetics may be viewed, to put it in his own words, as the fuller development of "that modern concept of poetry and art, which, inaugurated by Vico in the *Scienza Nuova,* and elaborated in various ways by classical German philosophy, was sharpened and popularized in Italy by the teaching of De Sanctis."[18] This is a neat historical statement on Croce's part, inasmuch as it brings to the fore the three major sources of his philosophy of art: Giambattista Vico, German idealism, and Francesco De Sanctis. Let us deal with each of these sources briefly, beginning with that of German idealism from Kant to Hegel.

It is customary to label Croce a "neo-Hegelian" in philosophy, but the tag does not exactly fit him. The question is quite complicated, and I think that, of all the classical German philosophers, he is closest to Immanuel Kant (1724–1804) in spirit, if not in letter, especially with respect to the attitude taken

---

[17] Croce, *Proemio alla "Critica" nel suo XLII Anno* (Bari: Laterza, 1945), p. 7. See Croce, *History of Italy,* pp. 237–255, for the cultural background and editorial policy of his bimonthly, *La Critica.*

[18] *Primi saggi,* p. 172.

against traditional "Metaphysics" with a capital "M." In any case, whether Croce is neo-Hegelian or not depends, for one thing, not only on the period of his intellectual life being considered, but also on the subject involved. For example, as he himself confessed, at the time that he was Hegelian in theory of art, he was anti-Hegelian in theory of history.[19] Furthermore, even when he undertook a serious study of Hegel during the middle period of his life at Gentile's instigation, the immediate result was apparently to make him more consciously anti-Hegelian than he had been originally.[20]

This is not the occasion to discuss Croce's various ups and downs with the grandest of German philosophers, his proposed reform of the Hegelian dialectic, and his acute observations on the "living" and "dead" parts of Hegel's philosophy.[21] Suffice it to mention that Croce credits Hegel fully for emphasizing "the cognitive character of art more than his predecessors"[22] belonging to the post-Kantian idealistic tradition in Germany. But at the same time he maintains that the Hegelian aesthetic logically terminates in an obituary or "funeral eulogy" on the arts, since they cannot help but be swallowed, in the final analysis, by the panlogistic jaws of the Absolute. Still, all told, whatever systematic or architectonic virtue be possessed by the Crocian system itself is doubtless due in no small measure to that master architect of the intellect, Georg Hegel (1770–1831).

As to the relationship of Croce to De Sanctis (1817–1883), the literary critic and historian of the late nineteenth century generally acknowledged to be Italy's greatest, the early De Sanctis no doubt was a Hegelian of a sort in aesthetics, and to the extent that this is true, it could easily be argued that his unquestionable influence on Croce may at least serve as indirect evidence to support the popular interpretation of Crocianism as a contemporary Italian variant of Hegelianism. Yet, as Croce

19 *Ibid.*, p. 54.

20 See Croce's *Autobiography* for details on his intellectual relations with Hegel *et al.*

21 Croce wrote extensively on Hegel, only part of what he had to say on the subject appearing in *What is Living and What is Dead of the Philosophy of Hegel*, trans. Douglas Ainslie (London: Macmillan, 1915).

22 Croce, *Estetica*, pp. 336–337.

himself has made quite clear, De Sanctis originally was an ortho-
dox Hegelian, but "in the end" he "rebelled openly against
everything within Hegel that was artificial, formalistic, and pedantic."[23] If this is so, the implication is obvious: the influence
of Croce's "ideal master"[24] on him is less Hegelian in direction
than often presupposed.

At any rate, Croce learns from De Sanctis that the essence of
art lies in its "form,"[25] by which is meant not something abstracted from "content," but the transformation of any emotional state or content whatsoever into an object of contemplation or artistic vision. In other words, to elucidate with a famous
example from De Sanctis himself, Croce learns that the gods of
Homer may be dead as an article of faith, but that the *Iliad* still
lives on as a work of art. This lesson was to provide him ultimately with the key to resolve, to his satisfaction, the "Form-
versus-Content" debate in modern aesthetics. To anticipate the
argument presented in the *Breviario,* the Crocian resolution of
the debate between the *formalisti* ("formalists") and the *con-
tenutisti* ("content-ists") in aesthetics (between the Herbartians
and the Hegelians, respectively), rests on the assumption that
every genuine work of art is actually a concrete "synthesis" of
both form and content in the abstract. Here, by the way, Croce
is definitely *neo*-Hegelian. For, even though he applies the dia-
lectical method to the aesthetics of form and content, the two
polar terms of the synthesis—form and content—are not inter-
preted as "opposites" à la Hegel, but as "distincts," inasmuch
as the emotional content of a work of art has an abstract status
only when viewed aesthetically, but certainly not when viewed
emotionally. And to the extent that he applies the principle of
polarity with unusual consistency, Croce definitely goes beyond
De Sanctis, who was more a man of letters than a philosopher
in the strict sense.

Of the three formative sources of Croce's aesthetic ideas
which he specifically acknowledges—Vico, German idealism,
and De Sanctis—I think it would be correct to say that Croce

23 *Ibid.,* p. 403.
24 *Ibid.,* p. xiv.
25 *Ibid.,* pp. 408–410.

as a literary critic is indebted most of all to Francesco De Sanctis, but that as a philosopher of art his greatest debt is to Giambattista Vico. Accordingly, at the risk of oversimplification, let me suggest in this connection that the philosophical label which perhaps best fits Croce (in aesthetics at least) is "neo-Vichian," rather than "neo-Hegelian." In short, Croce is the new Vico of aesthetics in Italy. What is some of the evidence for this thesis?

To begin with, let us recall what is worth repeating, to wit, that Vico for Croce is the Father of Aesthetics as a modern science, although Baumgarten is the first to christen it with that felicitous name. But, as if this tribute to that solitary voice in the wilderness during the Age of Intellect (not the "Age of Reason" for Croce) were not enough, Vico is also for him "the father of modern European philosophy"[26]—an honor traditionally reserved for Descartes. However, even though "the keen, restless, and stormy" author of the *Scienza Nuova* is "commonly treated as the inventor of the Philosophy of history,"[27] Croce holds that Vico's "New Science" is really *"Aesthetics."*[28] Thus, in a word, Vico is the Columbus of the New World of Aesthetics. Now, whether such interpretation is faithful to Vico's work or not is immaterial. For the crucial point for our thesis is that it constitutes *Croce's* Vico, than whom no greater aesthetician exists in the whole history of philosophy. But, if this is the case, what makes Croce the *new* Vico in aesthetics? The answer should be perfectly obvious.

After the twentieth-century disciple pays his twofold tribute to Vico, as indicated above, Croce then proceeds in characteristic fashion to point out the "errors"[29] of his real intellectual

26 Croce, *History of Italy,* p. 245.

27 Croce, *Estetica,* p. 255.

28 *Ibid.,* p. 256.

29 *Ibid.,* pp. 256–258. It is worth comparing Croce's chapter on Vico in *Estetica,* pp. 242–258, with its counterpart in Croce, *The Philosophy of Giambattista Vico,* trans. R. G. Collingwood (London: Howard Latimer, 1913), pp. 44–61, where a more critical approach to Vico's aesthetic ideas is to be found, and where even his tribute to Vico as the discoverer of the "New Science" of Aesthetics is made "with the reservations to which the determination of discoveries and discoverers is always subject" (p. 46).

master. Chief of these, as far as aesthetics proper is concerned, is Vico's tendency to confuse the theoretical problem as to the nature of poetry and art with the historical problem as to their actual origins in human civilization. As a consequence of this "confusion" of two different problems, Vico is led unfortunately to identify poetry as the "auroral" form of the human spirit with "barbarism" as the initial stage of civilization. Still, despite Vico's antiquated mistakes (which are regarded as minor in comparison with his novel insights), Croce concludes, in a positive vein, that the modern mind owes "the discovery of the autonomy of the aesthetic world" to "the genius of Giambattista Vico."[30]

To summarize Croce's intellectual relations to Vico, it may be said that Croce sees himself essentially as a sympathetic expurgator and more consistent continuator of Vico in aesthetics.[31] Taking as point of departure Vico's "bold and revolutionary innovation" that poetry represents "the imaginative form of knowledge" logically "prior to intellect and free from reflection and reasoning,"[32] Croce was to arrive at the all-important conclusion that there are not just one but two relatively autonomous forms of knowledge: (1) a simple or intuitive form and (2) a complex or conceptual form—each of which enjoys a cognitive or "theoretical value" of its own. And calling attention at the beginning of the twentieth century to the need "of conceiving the new aesthetics as Vico did at the beginning of the eighteenth," Croce was to develop his own theory of aesthetics as a "Logic of *intuition or representation* side by side with the Logic of the intellect,"[33] by clarifying Vico's key notion of "the Logic of Poetry,"[34] generalizing it into the logic of art as a whole. Finally, as a corollary of Vico's far-reaching idea that poetry and language are "substantially identical,"[35] Croce was to infer the actual identity of aesthetics as "the science of expression"

---

[30] *Ibid.,* p. 258.
[31] *Ibid.,* p. 258.
[32] Croce, *Philosophy of Giambattista Vico,* pp. 47, 55.
[33] Croce, *Primi saggi,* p. 183.
[34] Croce, *Philosophy of Giambattista Vico,* p. 47.
[35] Croce, *Estetica,* p. 247.

with "general linguistics"—an inference, incidentally, which might well be of interest, and even of benefit, to students of language analysis at present, whether of the Oxford variety or not.

IV. ORGANIC UNITY OF CROCE'S AESTHETICS, AND ITS CHALLENGERS

In view of the fact that Croce pondered the problems of aesthetics for some sixty years and kept writing about them continuously, Croce scholars have had the terrific problem of keeping pace with the development of his ideas on the subject. Some have exploited the situation (a few perhaps with malice) and have exaggerated the changes in his theory of art, questioning the logical unity of his aesthetic thought and going so far as to speak rather glibly of the existence of no less than three[36] or four[37] aesthetics in his writing. Croce himself, who had such a keen sense of human history and, naturally, an even keener sense of his own history, to be sure, repeatedly acknowledged in print the "elaborations" he made of his own aesthetic, but he never meant these *svolgimenti,* such as the defense of the

[36] For the interpretation (or, to be more exact, the misinterpretation) of the "three aesthetics" in Croce, see Adriano Tilgher, *Estetica: teoria generale dell'attività artistica* (Rome: Libreria di Scienze e Lettere, 1931), pp. 18–19. Cf. also Gherardo Marone, "Estética y Método Crítico en Italia desde G. B. Vico hasta B. Croce," in B. Croce, *Aesthetica in nuce,* trans. Italia Questa De Marelli (Buenos Aires: Inter-Americana, 1943), pp. 73–90.

[37] For the interpreters of at least four aesthetics in Croce, see Gian N. G. Orsini, *Benedetto Croce: Philosopher of Art and Literary Critic* (Carbondale: Southern Illinois University Press, 1961), p. 6. Cf. Angelo A. De Gennaro, *The Philosophy of Benedetto Croce: An Introduction* (New York: Philosophical Library, 1961), p. 24. It should be added that these two men seem to agree on the different varieties of aesthetics in Croce, but not exactly as to what they are specifically! Out of fairness it should also be added that one of them (Orsini) admits at the outset, "It may perhaps be excessive to speak of four different doctrines" (Orsini, p. 6) in Croce's writings on aesthetics, but then he proceeds as if they really are there. This scholar, who is very sympathetic to Croce's contributions to aesthetics and literary criticism, writes a whole well-documented volume on the subject, but one based on a false premise.

"lyrical" and the "universal or cosmic" qualities of art, to be taken as, in any way, departures from his central doctrine of art as pure expression or intuition, expounded in his magnum opus of 1902, *Estetica*.[38] Besides, those Croce critics and scholars who see three or four aesthetics in his work, seem to forget that philosophers as a rule are a pretty stubborn lot and hardly ever change their minds on fundamentals once they have arrived at them upon considerable reflection. If this is generally the case with philosophers as a class, it is actually even more so with Croce, who never wavered from the thesis of the cognitive significance of art (in the intuitive sense), and never yielded to its ever-popular alternative, which stresses art's purely emotive significance. Had he yielded, his entire system of philosophy, and not merely its aesthetic component, would have completely collapsed. So much for the obvious.

A careful and dispassionate examination of Croce's work in aesthetics will reveal concretely that, from a strict philosophical standpoint, the development of his aesthetic thought from, say, 1893 until his death in 1952 exhibits a remarkable continuity, representing as it does in the main, logically speaking, simply a series of variations on the same theme, rather than substantial changes in doctrine, notwithstanding appearances to that effect. Moreover, these variations do not constitute, strictly speaking, "distinct phases in Croce's thinking"[39] on the problems of aesthetics; on the contrary, they constitute different *emphases* he gives to his favorite subject, in response to changing circumstances, including, of course, the challenge of his many critics, friendly and otherwise. These emphases in turn provide him with an opportunity to make explicit or clearer what had been left implicit or unclear in the earlier versions of his thoughts on the subject. To show that this is what our author is really

[38] See, for instance, Croce's fifth edition of the *Estetica* (Bari: Laterza, 1922), p. vii, where he refers to these particular characteristics of art as "the two principal elaborations" he had made of his pivotal concept of art as *intuizione*—a concept which (he makes it his business to underscore) "I have never had any reason whatsoever to abandon, because it has proven itself to me to be sound and workable."

[39] Orsini, p. 6.

doing in pointing from time to time to the "elaborations" of his doctrine, we are going to take a quick look at the very two writings of his appealed to by those who challenge the unity of his aesthetic thought and claim that there are at least three or four aesthetics in his work over the years.

In 1908, at the International Congress of Philosophy held at Heidelberg, Croce gave a paper (now classic) entitled (in English) "Pure Intuition and the Lyrical Nature of Art."[40] The author recognized the importance of this paper as a further clarification of his concept of aesthetic intuition, and actually said so in his Foreword to the fifth edition of *Estetica* (1922).[41] Nevertheless, this does not mean, as one of the interpreters of the multiple doctrines of aesthetics in Croce has argued recently, that in the Heidelberg paper "Croce formally introduces an alteration in his previous doctrine. He makes what he calls a philosophic deduction of the lyrical character of art from his previously formulated concept of pure intuition."[42] Now then, Croce certainly does that very thing, but a logical deduction of a doctrine is no "alteration" of it. Far from it, and this is confirmed empirically by what Croce himself has to say on the subject in the *Breviario* itself, where he states emphatically that the term "lyrical" is "redundant," serving only an "explanatory and polemical function"—it being just another "synonym" of "intuition."

The same negative conclusion may be reached if we take the second of the two writings exploited by those who argue for the multiplicity of aesthetic doctrines in Croce, namely, "The Character of Totality of Artistic Expression," published in the original in his journal in 1918 and elsewhere in English the same year.[43] Here again the claim is made that in this article, "Croce

---

[40] In Croce, *Aesthetic: Science of Expression and General Linguistic*, trans. Douglas Ainslie (London: Macmillan, 1909), pp. 371–403.

[41] See n. 38.

[42] Orsini, p. 47.

[43] Croce, "Il Carattere di Totalità dell'Espressione Artistica," *La Critica*, XVI (1918), 129–140; "The Character of Totality of Artistic Expression," English trans., Douglas Ainslie, *The English Review*, XXVI (June 1918), 475–486.

added another concept to his aesthetic: the 'cosmic' or universal character of art"—a concept which, if "taken literally, reverses the main direction of his earlier doctrine, which was entirely oriented towards the individuality of art and its cognition of the particular."[44] "However," the same challenger of the internal consistency of the Crocian doctrines on art is quick to add, "Croce's reversal was not complete and unqualified."[45] But the truth of the matter is that Croce's comparatively new accent on the "intuitive universality"[46] of art, as a criterion for distinguishing good from poor art, was no "reversal" at all from a logical standpoint, but only a dialectically necessary complement to his earlier stress on the intuitive individuality of art. Proof of this, once more, comes from Croce, and precisely from the very article to which the upholders of the three or four aesthetics in his career resort for their case against the organic unity of his philosophy of art.

In the 1918 essay on the universal quality of art, Croce makes the following declaration as a warning to those critics who even then accused him of eclecticism in aesthetics: "We have never felt the necessity of going outside the principle of the pure intuition, in order to understand the character of totality with which it is stamped, nor of introducing corrections, or, worse still, eclectical additions. It has sufficed us to remain confined within its limits, indeed to observe them with greater rigour, to plunge into it more deeply within those limits, and to extract the inexhaustible riches that this form of knowledge contains."[47] The implication of this most telling passage should be perfectly clear. The concept of the "universal or cosmic character" of art is no eclectic addition to the Crocian first principle of aesthetic intuition, and certainly no "reversal" of it: it is a logical explication of another of its aspects. This is precisely

[44] Orsini, p. 210.

[45] *Ibid.*, p. 210.

[46] Croce, "The Character of Totality of Artistic Expression," p. 480. Note should be taken that the "universality" of art for Croce is still *intuitive* in nature, hence different from ordinary or conceptual universality.

[47] *Ibid.*, p. 476.

what Croce attempts to demonstrate in the essay under consideration.

As to the historical reason for the shift of emphasis, on Croce's part, from the individualistic aspect of art to its universalistic aspect, the 1918 essay itself is quite revelatory. After explaining the deplorable state of the literary arts in the modern world and complaining of the bad influence of Rousseau upon them, the author pointedly asks: "But now, after a century and a half of romanticism, would it not be worth while, perhaps, if Aesthetics were to give greater emphasis to the doctrine of the cosmic or integral character of artistic truth?"[48] No matter where we stand with respect to this delicate issue, the so-called "new doctrine" of "cosmic intuition" [49] plainly furnishes no real evidence for those who are searching desperately for the "three" or "four" aesthetics in Croce.

In the light of the preceding considerations, we may conclude that there is just *one* system of aesthetics in Croce: an organic system of aesthetic intuitionism, all of one piece but, at the same time, of course, possessed of variety in unity. Consequently, that work of his which is of special interest to us here, *Breviario di estetica*, "provides a vivid summing up of Croce's thought," not only "up to 1912,"[50] as is obvious chronologically, but also since 1912. This takes us directly to the *Breviario*, its origin as a literary piece and its significance in contemporary philosophy.

V. PHILOSOPHICAL SIGNIFICANCE OF CROCE'S *Breviario*

Of the sixty or so books that Croce wrote and published during his lifetime, the *Breviario* is the one whose origin is directly connected with this country. In the Foreword to the Italian edition of the work, he refers fondly to it as "my American lectures."[51] The reason for this curious reference is that Croce had

---

48 Croce, "Il Carattere di Totalità dell'Espressione Artistica," reprinted in *Filosofia, Poesia, Storia* (Milan: Ricciardi, 1951), p. 243.

49 Orsini, p. 211.

50 *Ibid.*, p. 53.

51 Croce, *Breviario di estetica: quattro lezioni*, 12th ed. (Bari: Laterza, 1954), p. 3.

originally been invited to deliver them as part of the formal
inauguration of Rice Institute (now Rice University) in 1912.
This also explains why the subtitle of the *Breviario* is *Quattro
lezioni*. Croce did not actually deliver the "Four Lectures" in
person at Rice; he sent the manuscript instead.

In the Foreword to the *Breviario,* Croce remarks that his lectures were intended to serve "as an orientation on the chief problems of Aesthetics,"[52] and he repeats the point at the beginning
of the text itself. (This is one reason why the present translator
has entitled the *Breviario* in English, *Guide to Aesthetics*—the
other reason being that "breviary" is now used primarily as an
ecclesiastical term.) Moreover, in the same Foreword the author
acknowledges—which is so revealing as to warrant quoting in
full—that in the *Breviario* he has "not only abridged the most
important concepts" of his "previous volumes on the same
theme," but has "also expounded them with more coherence
and greater perspicuity"[53] than in his *Estetica* of 1902. Therefore, Croce's *Guide to Aesthetics* is, admittedly, not only the
large *Estetica* writ small, but writ better, insofar as it brings
together neatly the theoretical and historical ramifications of
the subject which had been separated somewhat artificially,
though intentionally, in the celebrated work of 1902. Furthermore, *Guide to Aesthetics* is not only the best introduction to
Croce's philosophy of art. It is in addition the best brief statement of his entire philosophy. Published in 1913, the *Breviario*
is already a little classic in aesthetics—perhaps the only contemporary work of its scope to have achieved that status in the
field.

Since Croce in *Guide to Aesthetics* discusses the place of art in
human life and how it fits in with the rest of our experience,
it might be helpful in that connection if we gave a thumbnail
sketch of his philosophical system, which goes under several
names, such as "Philosophy of Spirit," "absolute spiritualism,"
and "absolute historicism."[54]

[52] *Ibid.,* p. 1.
[53] *Ibid.,* p. 1.
[54] Croce, *Filosofia, Poesia, Storia,* pp. 13–29.

According to Croce, the proper study of philosophy is the
story of mankind. As a consequence, philosophy is defined as
the "methodology of historiography."[55] The world of human
history, which is "*the* world" for him, is the stage where the
eternal "drama" of the spirit is enacted. The drama itself of
human life consists of four acts, and only four. But, in contrast
to the acts of an ordinary drama, the four acts played by the
human spirit do not come one after the other in time; in other
words, their sequence is purely ideal or theoretical. The four
acts themselves in the Crocian system constitute the four irre-
ducible coexisting "moments" or forms of the spirit, in terms
of which the various aspects or levels of man's spiritual activities
are made intelligible.

The spiritual forms are conceived dialectically, that is, as
four phases or stages of development which mutually involve
each other. The first phase of the spirit corresponds to its aesthetic form, the second to its logical, the third to its economic, and
the fourth to its ethical. As to their reciprocal relationship to
each other, Croce symbolizes it in the *Breviario* as a "circle"
moving (after Vico) in cycles that occur and recur in history, not
as a "cusp"[56] terminating in a culminating point—"cusp" being
the term he employs to symbolize, for example, the Hegelian
interpretation of history, which culminates in the Absolute of
Philosophy itself.

For Croce, man is both a knower and a doer. As human knowledge manifests itself in two "distinct" forms, so does human
conduct. On the theoretical plane, man not only lives by reasoning, he also lives by intuiting, that is, by producing images and
enjoying them for their own sweet sakes. This being the case,
knowledge may have as its object either particulars (images),
which are the products of intuition (art), or universals (concepts), which are the products of reasoning (logic). Correspond-
ingly, on the practical plane, man lives not only by moral
promptings, but also by economic incentives. Hence, human
conduct may have as its objective either the satisfaction of needs

55 *Ibid.*, p. 29.
56 *Ibid.*, p. 71.

which are particular in reach (economics) or the satisfaction of those which are universal (ethics). If it is asked why man is a doer as well as a knower, Croce's answer is that the human soul is dissatisfied with mere knowledge and longs for action. It is such "dissatisfaction" that makes for the drama of human life. Parenthetically, it should be added that the Crocian system subsumes philosophy and historiography under logic, while the entire gamut of human emotions in their raw or vital state, plus the domains of economics (in the narrow sense), politics and law, and the mathematical and natural sciences, are subsumed interestingly enough under the economic form of the practical spirit.

Perhaps the two most original features of Croce's system of philosophy are those which have to do, on the one hand, with his insistence on artistic intuition as a *legitimate* species of knowledge and, on the other, with his equal insistence on the mathematical and natural sciences as its *illegitimate* species. Let us make a comment or two about each of these unique traits of the Crocian system.

Ever since Aristotle argued that no knowledge is possible without universals, there has been a serious doubt among thinkers as to whether a knowledge of particulars as such really qualifies for cognitive status. Croce is fully aware of this "intellectualistic" bias of Western thought, but he contends that "intuitive knowledge" *is* knowledge all right, though he admits candidly that it does not enjoy the same cognitive status as "conceptual knowledge," which operates with "concrete universals." As a matter of fact, his whole plea for artistic intuition rests on his firm belief in its cognitive significance. That is to say, Croce really believes that artistic intuition, whose objects are particulars (images) as against universals (concepts), enjoys truth-value. To illustrate, he is convinced that the image of, say, Iago in *Othello* is not just a fanciful concoction on Shakespeare's part, but a superb instance of intuition or "artistic truth." Therefore, Croce would agree with that famous line from *Ode on a Grecian Urn* that "Beauty is truth, truth beauty," though he would completely disagree with Keats that "that is all ye know on earth, and all ye need to know." Now, if this is all that Croce means by artistic truth or intuition—and what he means sounds pretty reasonable on examination, namely, that what is artistically true (or beautiful) is whatever is well expressed, and what is artistically false (or ugly) is whatever is poorly expressed—why is it that his aesthetics of intuition has been either unduly neglected or severely criticized, let alone highly misunderstood, especially in the English-speaking world? I submit three possible reasons for this rather unfortunate outcome of his appeal to intuition in aesthetics.

One reason is given by Croce himself, to repeat, the "intellectualistic" prejudice of Western philosophy against anything that smacks of "intuition," a weasel term (if there ever was one!) whose meanings in the history of ideas are notoriously legion. I strongly suspect that if Croce had substituted another less ambiguous and less controversial term in his theory of art to convey man's image-making power, and had made it perfectly clear that the "truths" of art lie in nothing but their peculiar mode of expression, pure and simple, he would have received a better hearing in intellectual circles. In any event, a second reason for the unfavorable reception of Croce's aesthetics in some circles may be taken from our own John Dewey, who contends that Croce approaches art in terms of "a preconceived system of philosophy," and so fails to understand it "in its own language."[57]

But thirdly and lastly, I think that the misunderstandings attending Croce's lot in aesthetics have been due, in the main, to his having been found, through no fault of his own, guilty by association with that exceedingly influential French philosopher in contemporary thought, Henri Bergson (1859-1941), who more than anyone else in the twentieth century put "intuition" back on the map of philosophy. Still, despite this unfortunate association, there is a world of difference between

[57] In P. Romanell, "A Comment on Croce's and Dewey's Aesthetics," *Journal of Aesthetics and Art Criticism*, VII (December 1949), 125. Needless to add, Dewey's critique of the Crocian aesthetic is not quite fair, but this is not the place to defend Croce against Dewey.

Croce's aesthetic concept of intuition in the *Estetica* (1902) and Bergson's metaphysical concept in *An Introduction to Metaphysics* (1903). The difference may be stated succinctly as follows: Whereas Bergson appeals to intuition as the key to metaphysical truth, Croce appeals to it as the key to artistic truth. Thus, there is no fusion (or confusion) of the two in Croce, no Bergsonian "aestheticism,"[58] simply because there is no such self-contradictory thing as "intellectual intuition" for him and, hence, no place for any metaphysic based thereon in his system. In contrast to Bergsonian intuition, Crocian intuition is restricted to the realm of art, where the distinction between reality and appearance, true and false in the ordinary sense, possible truth and actual truth, is irrelevant. In short, the doctrine of aesthetic intuitionism, which characterizes Part One of the Crocian System, puts intuition in the first moment of the spirit and keeps it there in its "pure" form as "artistic imagery."

If we pass from the first to the third moment of the spirit in the Crocian system, its other but more questionable feature will become apparent. It is here in the "economic" part of his system that Croce adds the useful (*economicità*) as a spiritual category to the traditional trinity of the beautiful, the true, and the good, and does so with the express purpose of redeeming a "condemned" concept in the history of ethics. The useful to him is not something to be ashamed of in life; in a word, it is not the unethical or egoistic *per se*. On the contrary, it stands for the utilitarian or hedonistic aspect of life—an aspect which, in Croce's eyes, is just as much part and parcel of life as the ethical.

Significantly enough, the fact that Croce does not neglect the utilitarian side of life in assigning it *a* place in his system doubtless reflects the early influence of Karl Marx on the formation of his mind.[59] On the other hand, the fact that he does not accord primacy to the utility factor at the expense of other

---

[58] Croce, *Logica come scienza del concetto puro*, 4th ed. (Bari: Laterza, 1920), p. 361.

[59] For Croce's early studies on Marxism, see his book, *Historical Materialism and the Economics of Karl Marx*, trans. C. M. Meredith (New York: Macmillan, 1914).

factors in life is proof that he is not a Marxist in theory. Finally, the dubious use that Croce makes of his Marx-inspired concept of the useful affects his interpretation of the mathematical and natural sciences. Exploiting the pragmatic doctrines of such empirio-criticists in the late nineteenth century as Richard Avenarius and Ernst Mach, who reduced all human thought to "economy," Croce ingeniously reduces not *all* our thought, but solely its mathematical and scientific varieties, to the same factor. Armed with this factor, he formulates an economic interpretation of the mathematical and natural sciences, claiming with Bergson (and here the two otherwise contrastable contemporary philosophers are in perfect accord) that, though their "pseudoconcepts" are undoubtedly useful in life, they are devoid of truth-value precisely on account of their mere utility. Like Kant of old, who clipped the wings of reason to make room for faith, so Croce reduces pure mathematics and natural science to their practical or technological value in order to make room for the theoretical or disinterested value of philosophy. Evidently, this is how Croce subtly takes his final revenge on Positivism as the Gospel of Science![60]

PATRICK ROMANELL

[60] For an account of the Crocian approach to the sciences, see P. Romanell, "Romanticism and Croce's Conception of Science," *Review of Metaphysics*, IX (March 1956), 505–514.

Selected Bibliography

Because of the extensiveness of the Crocian bibliography, it has been decided not only to omit Croce's contributions to literary criticism but also to restrict the list of his writings to those four volumes which make up his philosophical system, "Philosophy of Spirit." For the same reason, the collateral reading list omits journal articles and, moreover, is limited to pertinent books in English only.

CROCE'S MAJOR PHILOSOPHICAL WORKS

IN ITALIAN

Estetica come scienza dell'espressione e linguistica generale. Milan: Sandron, 1902.

Logica come scienza del concetto puro. Bari: Laterza, 1909.

Filosofia della pratica: economica ed etica. Bari: Laterza, 1909.

Teoria e storia della storiografia. Bari: Laterza, 1917.

IN ENGLISH

Aesthetic: Science of Expression and General Linguistic. Translated by DOUGLAS AINSLIE. London: Macmillan, 1909.

Philosophy of the Practical: Economic and Ethic. Translated by DOUGLAS AINSLIE. London: Macmillan, 1913.

Logic as the Science of the Pure Concept. Translated by DOUGLAS AINSLIE. London: Macmillan, 1917.

Theory & History of Historiography. Translated by DOUGLAS AINSLIE. London: G.G. Harrap, 1921.

COLLATERAL READING

BOSANQUET, B. *Croce's Aesthetic.* London: Oxford University Press, 1920.

CARR, H. W. *The Philosophy of Benedetto Croce.* London: Macmillan, 1917.

DE GENNARO, A. A. *The Philosophy of Benedetto Croce: An Introduction.* New York: Philosophical Library, 1961.

NARDO, G. J. *The Aesthetics of Benedetto Croce: A Critical Evaluation of Its Terminology and Internal Consistency.* Ann Arbor: University Microfilms, 1957.

ORSINI, G. N. G. *Benedetto Croce: Philosopher of Art and Literary Critic.* Carbondale: Southern Illinois University Press, 1961.

PICCOLI, R. *Benedetto Croce: An Introduction to His Philosophy.* London: J. Cape, 1922.

POWELL, A. E. *The Romantic Theory of Poetry: An Examination in the Light of Croce's Aesthetic.* New York: Russell & Russell, 1962.

ROMANELL, P. *Croce versus Gentile: A Dialogue on Contemporary Italian Philosophy.* New York: S. F. Vanni, 1946.

SEERVELD, C. G. *Benedetto Croce's Earlier Aesthetic Theories and Literary Criticism: A Critical Philosophical Look at the Development During His Rationalistic Years.* Kampen, The Netherlands, 1958.

SPRIGGE, C. J. S. *Benedetto Croce: Man and Thinker.* New Haven: Yale University Press, 1952.

STRUCKMEYER, O. K. *Croce and Literary Criticism.* Cambridge, England: R. I. Severs, 1921.

WIMSATT, W. K., and BROOKS, C. *Literary Criticism: A Short History.* New York: Knopf, 1957.

Note on the Text

Croce's *Breviario di estetica* made its first appearance in English under one title, and about a decade later a slightly revised edition was published under another title. Both were by the same translator, Douglas Ainslie.[1] Although it is unfortunately true, as one Croce scholar has frankly put it, that "Ainslie's translations of Croce are notoriously faulty,"[2] we should all be grateful just the same to that Scottish poet for making the major philosophical works of his new "Columbus" available to the English-speaking world, on the ground that even a poor translation of Croce, hypothetically, may be better than none at all, and further that the Italian philosopher is no easy author to translate into any language anyway, let alone into English. Croce's sentences, in the *Breviario* at least, are much too long for current English taste, and his thought at times gets a bit involved. Consequently, in order to convey the meaning of his thought as faithfully as possible, in the present translation I have taken the liberty of shortening his sentences and changing his paragraphs accordingly, when absolutely necessary. With the same goal in mind, I have taken the additional liberty of adding in brackets a word here or a phrase there. There is only one footnote in the original; all the rest have been added to elucidate the text.

The author of *Guide to Aesthetics* does such an excellent job of summarizing his case for aesthetic intuitionism that it would seem superfluous to summarize his summary. Even so readers in the English-speaking world must be forewarned of Croce's par-

1 Benedetto Croce, *The Breviary of Aesthetic,* in *The Book of the Opening of The Rice Institute,* II (Houston: The Rice Institute, 1912), 430–517; *The Essence of Aesthetic* (London: Heinemann, 1921).

2 Gian N. G. Orsini, *Benedetto Croce: Philosopher of Art and Literary Critic* (Carbondale: Southern Illinois University Press, 1961), p. 304.

ticular use of the terms *fantasia* and *immaginazione* in the body of the text itself. Following a terminology derived directly from De Sanctis and indirectly from Schelling and Hegel,[3] Croce uses *fantasia* to signify "fancy" in the good or poetic sense, and *immaginazione* to signify "imagination" in the bad or mechanical sense. The distinction does not, to be sure, correspond to present-day English usage, the meaning of the two terms having been reversed. However, in order to be faithful to the text, I have kept the distinction to conform to Croce's own usage; I hope that the context itself will disclose exactly in what sense the two terms in question are to be understood.

Needless to mention, the title of the first lecture of the *Breviario* is a reference to Tolstoy's *What is Art?* (1898). Croce begins his treatise with Tolstoy's question but, ironically, answers it in a way that, despite appearances to the contrary, is diametrically opposite to the position taken by the famous Russian writer. If we know Croce at all, the irony was fully intended.

The present translation is based on the twelfth edition of Benedetto Croce's *Breviario di estetica* (Bari: Laterza, 1954), pp. 5–102.

P. R.

---

[3] Croce, *Estetica* (6th. ed.), p. 403.

GUIDE TO AESTHETICS

I. "What Is Art?"

To the question, "What is art?," one could reply in jest—and it would not be a foolish retort—that art is something everybody knows about. As a matter of fact, had we not some inkling already as to what art is, the question itself could not even be raised. For every question entails some notion of what is being asked, implicit in the question and, therefore, qualified and known. This is actually confirmed by the accurate and profound ideas which are often heard expressed about art by those who make no profession of philosophy or theory—laymen, artists (who are no lovers of reasoning), naïve persons, and even by the masses. At times these ideas are implicit in the judgments uttered concerning single works of art, but on other occasions they assume explicitly the form of aphorisms and definitions. Apropos of this, it would be possible (provided we so desired) to embarrass every proud philosopher, who fancies himself to have "discovered" the nature of art, by placing before his eyes and making resound in his ears certain statements written in the most familiar books or certain phrases of the most ordinary conversation, and showing him that these statements and phrases already contain all too plainly the discovery of which he boasts.

Moreover, the philosopher in this instance would have sufficient cause to be embarrassed if, that is, he had ever entertained the illusion that, by means of his own doctrines, he could introduce into human consciousness in general something altogether original of his own, extraneous to that consciousness, the revelation of an entirely new world. Yet he is not disconcerted and proceeds merrily on his way. For he is not unaware that the question as to the nature of art (and for that matter, every philosophical question regarding the nature of the real, or, in general, all questions about knowledge) has always, in fact, a *circumstantial* meaning—referring as it does to the particular diffi-

3

culties that come to life at a specific moment in the history of thought—even though because of the words employed the question itself takes on the aspect of a general or universal problem which one pretends to solve once and for all.

To be sure, truth walks the streets, like the *esprit* in the well-known French proverb, or like the metaphor—"queen of tropes," according to the rhetoricians—which Montaigne[a] used to keep finding in the *babil* of his *chambrière*.[1] But, the metaphor of the chambermaid is itself the solution to a problem of expression, peculiar to the feelings which throb in her at that moment. The obvious assertions regarding the nature of art, which are heard daily either accidentally or intentionally, are themselves solutions to logical problems, such as they appear to this or that individual who is not a philosopher by profession, and yet who, by virtue of being a man, is himself a philosopher too, in some measure. And just as the chambermaid's metaphor usually expresses but a narrow and poor range of feelings compared with the poet's, so the obvious assertion of the non-philosopher solves a problem trivial by comparison with that which the philosopher proposes to himself.

The answers as to what art is may look the same in appearance in both cases, but are different in fact, owing to the difference of richness in their internal content. The answer of the philosopher worthy of the name has precisely the task of solving adequately all the problems which have arisen, down to that moment in the course of history, concerning the nature of art. On the other hand, the answer of the layman, operating within much narrower limits, turns out to be powerless outside of those limits. Empirical evidence for this difference may be found in the power of the eternal Socratic method, in the ease with which the learned, with their barrage of questions, leave confused and agape the uninformed, who likewise start off by making sense but who, on running the risk during the course of the discussion of losing even the little knowledge in their possession, have no other recourse than to retreat into their own shell, declaring that they are not fond of "subtleties."

[a] [Notes indicated by letters appear in the Appendix, pp. 83–88.]
[1] [Michel de Montaigne, *Essais*, I (Paris: Garnier, 1952), 340.]

Here alone, then, is where the pride of the philosopher has its place, to wit, in his consciousness of the greater scope of his questions and answers. However, this pride is not unaccompanied with modesty; that is, there is awareness that, even though the philosopher's approach to things is broader, or the broadest possible at a determinate moment, it nevertheless still has its limits (those traced by the history of that moment), and thus cannot pretend to complete validity nor be, as they say, a *definitive* solution. The subsequent life of the spirit, by renewing and multiplying problems, makes preceding solutions not so much false as inadequate, some of which fall into the group of those truths that are understood implicitly, while others need to be reconsidered and integrated.

A system of thought is like a house which, right after being built and decorated, requires for its upkeep an effort more or less vigorous but assiduous (subject as it is to the corroding action of the elements). Now, at a certain moment it is no longer worth repairing and propping but must be demolished and started from scratch. Yet there is, to be exact, this major difference between the two, namely, in the work of thought, the perpetually new house is perpetually maintained by the old one— which, almost through a feat of magic, persists in the new. As is obvious, those who are ignorant of the magic in question— the superficial or naïve minds—are frightened by it. So much so that one of their tiresome refrains against philosophy is that it continually undoes its own work, and that one philosopher contradicts another. As if man were not always making and unmaking and remaking his own houses, and the architect to follow were not the contradicter of his predecessor! And, as if from this making and unmaking and remaking of houses, and from this contradicting of each other on the part of architects, one could ever draw the conclusion that it is useless to build houses!

Coupled with their advantage of greater scope, the questions and answers of the philosopher also carry with them the risk of greater error, being as they are frequently vitiated by a sort of lack of common sense. But this lack, insofar as it pertains to a higher sphere of culture, has, even in its censurable aspects, an aristocratic character, object not only of scorn and ridicule, but also of secret admiration and envy. Be that as it may, herein lies the basis of the contrast, which many are delighted to bring out, between the mental equilibrium of ordinary people and the follies of the philosophers. For it is clear that no man of common sense would ever have said, for example, that art is the echo of the sexual instinct, or that art is a harmful thing deserving to be banished from well-governed states[b]—absurdities which philosophers, including great ones too, have uttered. Still, the innocence of the common-sense man represents penury, a primitive innocence. And although there has often been a longing for the innocent life of the savage, calling for a remedy to rescue common sense from philosophy, the fact remains that the spirit, in its development, faces with courage, as it must, the dangers of civilization and the momentary loss of common sense. The philosopher's investigation of art is obliged to wander over the paths of error in order to discover the paths of truth, which are not different from the paths of error, but those very same paths, except that they have been traversed with the help of a string which permits a way out of the labyrinth.

The strict relationship of error and truth originates from the fact that a pure or absolute error is inconceivable and, for this reason, does not exist. Error speaks with a double voice, one of which affirms the false, while the other belies it, thereby constituting that clash of yes and no which is called contradiction. Consequently, when we go from a general consideration to a detailed and specific examination of a theory which has been condemned as erroneous, we find in the theory itself the cure for its falsity, that is to say, the true theory which sprouts from the soil of error.

Thus, we learn that those very ones who boast of reducing art to the sexual instinct must, in order to demonstrate their thesis, resort to arguments and compromises which, instead of uniting art and that instinct, separate them. And we also learn that the man[2] who expelled poetry from well-ordered states used to tremble at the thought of doing so, and himself created, through

2 [Plato, *Republic* X. 607.]

that very act, a new sublime poetry. There have been historical periods in which the most perverse and crude doctrines of art prevailed. But these did not, even then, stand in the way of making the usual distinction, in the most reliable manner possible, between the beautiful and the ugly, and of reasoning quite neatly on the subject, especially when the abstract theory was forgotten and discussion turned to particular cases. Error is always condemned, not out of the judge's mouth, but *ex ore suo*.[3]

Because of this strict relationship with error, the assertion of truth is always a process of struggle, through which we free ourselves from error whenever we fall into it. Hence, another pious but unattainable wish is the one which requests that truth be disclosed directly, without discussion or polemic, letting it march on majestically all by itself. As if such stage paraphernalia were the symbol appropriate to truth, which is thought itself and, as such, is forever active and in travail! Indeed, no one succeeds in disclosing a truth except by criticism of the various solutions of the problem to which it refers. There is no philosophical treatise, however poor, no tiny student manual or academic dissertation, that does not include at the outset, or within the body of the text, a review of opinions (furnished by history, or theoretically possible) which it wishes to oppose and correct. This review, no matter how often it may be performed in an arbitrary and confused fashion, expresses precisely the legitimate need, in dealing with a problem, of going over all the solutions which were attempted in history or are attemptable in theory (that is, at the present moment, though still within history), so that the new solution may include within itself the preceding efforts of the human spirit.

However, the need just mentioned is a *logical* requirement and, as such, is intrinsic to every true thought and inseparable from it. Furthermore, it must not be confused with a special literary form of exposition, otherwise we fall into the pedantry with which the Schoolmen in the Middle Ages and the dialecticians of the Hegelian school in the nineteenth century made

3 ["From its own mouth."]

themselves famous, and which since is very much like the super-
stition of formalism, with its faith in the remarkable virtue of a
certain extrinsic and mechanical mode of philosophic exposition. In short, it is necessary to understand the need in a substantial (not accidental) sense, honoring the spirit and not the letter,
and proceeding in the exposition of one's own thought with free
rein, according to the times, places, and persons.

Therefore, in these cursory lectures which endeavor to provide
a sort of orientation on the method of treating problems of art,
I shall be careful to refrain from giving an account (as I have
done elsewhere) of the history of aesthetic thought, or from
explaining dialectically· (as I have also done elsewhere)ᶜ the
whole process of liberation from the erroneous conceptions of
art, from the poorest to the richest in ascending order. In addition, I shall dispose (not for myself but for my readers) of part
of the baggage with which they will load themselves later when,
under the spell of a bird's-eye view of the country, they can
fortify themselves to carry out more specialized trips to this or
that part of it, or travel over the whole of it part by part.

And now, to resume the question which gave occasion to this
indispensable prologue (that is, indispensable for removing
from my discussion any trace of pretentiousness as well as the
taint of its uselessness)—the question as to what art is—let me
answer it immediately and in the simplest manner: art is *vision*
or *intuition*. The artist produces an image or picture. The person who enjoys art turns his eyes in the direction which the
artist has pointed out to him, peers through the hole which
has been opened for him, and reproduces in himself the artist's
image. "Intuition," "vision," "contemplation," "imagination,"
"fancy," "invention," "representation," and so forth, are words
which continually reappear as almost synonymous in discussions
on art. All of them give rise in our minds to the same concept or
to the same set of concepts—a sign of universal consent.

But this answer of mine, that art is intuition, acquires significance as well as strength from all that it implicitly denies and
from which art is distinguished. What are the negations it in-
cludes? I shall indicate the chief ones, or at least those most
important for us at our present moment of culture.

The answer denies, above all, that art is a *physical* fact, as, for example, certain particular colors or combinations of colors, forms of the body, sounds or combinations of sounds, phenomena of heat or electricity—in brief, anything which goes under the name of "physical." This error of materializing art has already made a dent upon popular thought. Like children who touch the soap bubble and then yearn to touch the rainbow, the human spirit in its admiration of beautiful things is naturally inclined to trace its causes to external nature, and convinces itself to consider (or believes it ought to consider) some colors as beautiful and others as ugly, some forms of the body as beautiful and others as ugly. As a matter of fact, this attempt has been carried out intentionally and methodically many a time in the history of thought—from the "canons" which the artists and theorists of Greece and the Renaissance established for the beauty of bodies, and the speculations on the geometrical and numerical relations determinable for shapes and sounds, to the investigations of the aestheticians in the nineteenth century (for instance, Fechner's),[d] and the "papers" which the inexperienced usually present nowadays on the connections of physical phenomena with art, at our congresses of philosophy, psychology, and the natural sciences.

If it is asked why art cannot be a physical fact, it is necessary to state, first of all, that physical facts *lack reality*. On the other hand, art, to which so many devote their whole lives and which fills everyone with heavenly joy, is *supremely real*. Consequently, it cannot be a physical fact, which is something unreal. All of which doubtless sounds paradoxical at first, for nothing seems to the common man more firm and certain than the physical world. Nevertheless, from the standpoint of truth, we are not permitted to give up valid reasoning by substituting for it something less valid simply because the first has the semblance of falsehood.

Moreover, to overcome the strange and harsh sound of the truth in question or to become familiar with it, we should take into consideration that the proof of the unreality of the physical world has not only been established in an irrefutable way and is conceded by all philosophers (who are neither cross mate-

rialists nor involved in the strident contradictions of materialism), but that the proof itself is being acknowledged by the
physicists themselves—as evident in the traces of philosophy
which they mix in with their science—when they conceive
physical phenomena as manifestations of principles which go
beyond experience, such as the atoms or the ether, or as the
manifestation of an Unknowable. Besides, the very Matter of
the materialists is a supermaterial principle. Thus, physical
facts, by their internal logic and by common consent, make
themselves known not as something truly real, but as a *construction of our intellect for purposes of science*. Consequently, the
question as to whether art is a physical fact should rationally
assume another meaning, namely, whether art may *be constructed physically*.

This is certainly possible, and we actually do so whenever, on
diverting our attention from the sense of a poem, or on giving
up its enjoyment, we begin, say, to count the words of which the
poem is composed and divide them into syllables and letters.
Or whenever, on diverting our attention from the aesthetic
effect of a statue, we measure it and weigh it. To do so is, no
doubt, of the greatest utility to packers of statues, as to count
words is useful to printers who have to "compose" pages of
poetry! But it is utterly useless to the contemplator or student
of art, to whom it is not useful or permissible "to divert his attention" from his proper object. Not even, therefore, in this
second sense is art a physical fact, because when we undertake to
penetrate its nature and its mode of operation, it is of no avail
to make a physical thing out of it.

Another negation implicit in the definition of art as intuition
is that if art is intuition, and if intuition signifies *theory* in the
original sense of contemplation, then art cannot be a utilitarian
act. For, inasmuch as a utilitarian act aims always at arriving
at a pleasure and, hence, at removing a pain, art considered in
terms of its own nature has nothing to do with the *useful*, or
with *pleasure* and *pain*, as such.

It will be admitted in effect, without too much opposition,
that a pleasure as pleasure, any pleasure whatever, is not in itself

artistic. The pleasure from a drink of water which quenches our thirst is not artistic. Neither is a walk in the open air which stretches our limbs and makes our blood circulate more rapidly, nor is the attainment of a coveted post which results in lending security to our practical life, and so forth. Even in the relations which develop between ourselves and works of art, the difference between pleasure and art is self-evident. For the figure represented may be dear to us and awaken the most delightful memories, but the picture may be ugly, nevertheless. On the other hand, the picture may be beautiful, but the figure represented abominable to our soul. Or the picture itself, which we approve as beautiful, may provoke later a fit of rage and envy, owing to its being a work of an enemy or a rival, to whom it will bring certain advantages and renewed vigor. Our practical interests, with their correlative pleasures and pains, are blended, become confused now and then, and disquiet our aesthetic interest, but never become *united* with it.

At most, to defend on more valid grounds the definition of art as the pleasurable, one might argue that art is not the pleasurable in general but a *special* form of it. However, this restriction is no longer a defense but rather an actual abandonment of that thesis. For assuming that art is a special form of the pleasurable, it follows that its distinctive character would not be supplied by the pleasurable as such, but by whatever distinguishes the artistic from other forms of the pleasurable. And it is to that distinctive element apart from the pleasurable, or different from it, to which it would be fitting to address the inquiry. In any case, the doctrine which defines art as the pleasurable has a special name (hedonistic aesthetics), and is a long and complicated affair in the history of aesthetic theory. It appeared back in the Greco-Roman world, was prevalent in the eighteenth century, flourished again in the second half of the nineteenth century, and still meets with much approval, especially among beginners in aesthetics, who are primarily impressed with the fact that art arouses pleasure.

The career of this doctrine has consisted either in proposing from time to time this or that class of pleasures or several classes together (the pleasure of the higher senses, the pleasure of play, the consciousness of one's own strength, eroticism, etc.), or in adding elements other than the pleasurable, as, for example, the useful (when it used to be understood as something distinct from the pleasurable), the satisfaction of cognitive and moral needs, and the like. Progress has come about precisely because of its unstable nature, allowing as it has outside elements to ferment within its bosom—elements introduced by it out of necessity to bring itself somehow into harmony with the reality of art—thus reaching the point of dissolving itself as hedonistic doctrine and of promoting unconsciously a new doctrine, or, at least, of calling attention to the need of one. Now, since every error has its element of truth (that of the physical doctrine, as we have seen, is the possibility of the physical "construction" of art as of any other fact), the hedonistic doctrine has its eternal element of truth in placing in relief the hedonistic accompaniment, or pleasure. As pleasure is common to aesthetic activity and to every other form of spiritual activity, no denial of it is intended at all in denying categorically the identification of art with the pleasurable, and in distinguishing it from the pleasurable by defining it as intuition.

A third negation effected with the help of the theory of art as intuition is the denial of art as a *moral act*. In other words, it denies that art is that form of practical activity which, though necessarily associated with the useful and with pleasure and pain, is not immediately utilitarian and hedonistic, operating as it does on a higher spiritual plane. Even so, as theoretical activity, intuition is against anything practical. In fact, as has been observed from time immemorial, art does not originate from an act of will. Good will, which constitutes the honest man, does not constitute the artist. Moreover, since art is not born from an act of will, it likewise is not subject to any moral evaluation, not because an exemption privilege is accorded to it, but simply because no way is available to apply moral distinctions to it. An artistic image can depict a morally praiseworthy or blameworthy action. But the image itself, as such, is neither praiseworthy nor blameworthy, morally. Not only is there no penal code which can condemn an image to prison or to death, but no moral judgment passed by a reasonable person could ever address itself to it as its object. Otherwise, to judge Dante's Francesca immoral or Shakespeare's Cordelia moral (these perform a mere artistic function, being like musical notes within Dante's and Shakespeare's souls) would be just as valid as to judge a square moral or a triangle immoral.

Furthermore, the moralistic theory of art is also represented in the history of aesthetic doctrines and is not altogether dead even today, although it is much discredited in current opinion. However, it is discredited not only for its internal defect, but, in addition, to some extent, on account of the moral shortcomings of some present tendencies which facilitate, thanks to psychological jargon, that refutation which should be made—and which we are here doing—solely on logical grounds. From the moralistic doctrine is derived art's pre-established goal to serve as a guide to the good, inspire the abhorrence of evil, correct and improve manners and morals. And from the same source comes the demand that artists contribute to the public education of the lower classes, the reinforcing of the national or warlike spirit of a people, the spreading of the ideals of a modest and industrious life, and so on.

All of which are things that art cannot do, any more than can geometry, which, notwithstanding, does not lose any of its respectability on this account; and in view of this, one does not see why art should lose any of its, either. Even the moralistic aestheticians used to see dimly that art cannot do such things, and for this reason they quite willingly came to terms with it, allowing it also to extol pleasures that were not moral, provided that they were not openly offensive. They urged art to employ to good purposes the authority which it, through its hedonistic power, exercised over souls, such as sweetening bad news or sugar-coating the bitter pill. In short, they urged art, believe it or not, to play courtesan (because it had not managed to give up the old and natural habit), but at the service of the Holy Church or of morals! Moreover, at other times the moralistic aestheticians thought of making use of art as a didactic instrument, inasmuch as not only virtue but science too is exacting business. Art could remove that bad feature of it, and so make the entrance to the palace of science pleasant and attractive, nay, lead men to it as through a garden of Armida's[e]—merrily and voluptuously—without their being aware of the great benefit that they were receiving, and of the crisis of regeneration for which they were preparing themselves.

In talking about these theories, we today cannot refrain from smiling. However, we should not forget that they were a serious matter, corresponding as they did to an earnest effort to understand the nature of art and improve its concept. Besides, they had adherents whose names were (to restrict ourselves to Italian literature): Dante and Tasso, Parini[f] and Alfieri,[g] Manzoni[h] and Mazzini.[i] And even the moralistic theory of art was, and is, and will be perpetually beneficial, despite its very contradictions. It was, and is, and will be an effort, however unfortunate, to keep art separate from the merely pleasurable (with which it is sometimes confused), and assign to it a more fitting place. The moralistic doctrine has also its true side. For if art is beyond morals, the artist is not, since he is neither beyond nor this side of it, but under its dominion. Insofar as he is a man, the artist cannot shirk the duties of man and should consider art itself— which is not and never will be morals—as a mission, to be practiced like a priesthood.

Furthermore (and this is the last, and perhaps the most important, of the general negations which it suits my purposes to mention here), with the definition of art as intuition goes the denial that it has the character of *conceptual knowledge*. Conceptual knowledge in its pure form (which is that of the philosophical) is always oriented toward reality and aims to establish the real as distinguished from the unreal, or to diminish unreality in status by including it within reality as a subordinate part of itself. In contrast, intuition refers precisely to the lack of distinction between reality and unreality—to the image itself—with its purely ideal status as mere image.

The contrast being made here between intuitive or sensuous and conceptual or intellectual knowledge, between aesthetics and noetics, is aimed at restoring the autonomy of this simpler and elementary form of knowledge, which has been compared with the dream (dream, certainly not sleep) of the theoretical life, with respect to which philosophy would be the waking state. Accordingly, whoever before a work of art asks whether what the artist has expressed be metaphysically or historically true or false is asking a meaningless question, and falls into the error analogous to the one of the man who wants to bring before the tribunal of morality the ethereal images of fancy.

The question is meaningless because the distinction of true and false always concerns an assertion about reality, that is, a judgment, and thus is not applicable to the presentation of an image or to a mere subject—which is not the subject in a proposition, lacking as it does attribute or predicate. It is useless to object that the individual character of the image has no meaning without a reference to the universal, of which that image is its individuation. For here we certainly are not denying that the universal, like the spirit of God, is everywhere and animates everything from within itself. But we are denying that the universal is logically explicit or thought out in intuition as such. And likewise is it useless to appeal to the principle of the unity of the spirit, which is not weakened but rather strengthened by our precise distinction between fancy and thought, because only from distinction is opposition born, and concrete unity from opposition.

Ideality (as this property which distinguishes intuition from concept, art from philosophy and history, from assertion of the universal, and from perception or narration of events, has also been called) is the quintessence of art. As soon as reflection or judgment develops out of that state of ideality, art vanishes and dies. It dies in the artist, who changes from artist and becomes his own critic; it dies in the spectator or listener, who from rapt contemplator of art changes into a thoughtful observer of life.

Moreover, the distinction between art and philosophy (the latter understood in its broad sense, comprising every consideration of the real) carries with it other distinctions, of which there is, in the first place, the distinction between art and *myth*. To the one who believes in it, myth manifests itself as the revelation and knowledge of reality as opposed to unreality, along with a rejection of alternative beliefs as illusory and false. Myth can become art only to the person who does not believe in it any longer and avails himself of mythology as a metaphor, of the austere world of the gods as a beautiful world, of God as an image of the sublime. Considered then, metaphysically, in the mind of the believer (certainly not of the disbeliever), myth is religion and not pure fancy; and religion is philosophy—philosophy in process, philosophy more or less perfected, but still philosophy—just as philosophy is religion, more or less purified and elaborated, in continual process of elaboration and purification, but still religion or thought of the Absolute or the Eternal. What art lacks in order to be myth or religion is precisely thought, and the faith that springs from it. The artist neither believes nor disbelieves in his image; he produces it.

In addition, but for a different reason, the concept of art as intuition excludes the conception of art as the production of *classes, types, species, and genera,* or even (to refer to what a great mathematician and philosopher[j] had to say of music) as an unconscious exercise in *arithmetic.*[4] Accordingly art is distinguished from the positive and mathematical sciences, in both of which the conceptual form has a place—though one deprived of realistic status—as mere general representation or mere abstraction. Needless to add, that character of ideality, which the natural and mathematical sciences appear to assume as against the world of philosophy, religion, and history, and which seems to bring them closer to art (and owing to which the scientists and mathematicians of our day are so eager to brag about being creators of worlds, of *fictiones*—a term similar, even as far as language is concerned, to the one designating the tales or inventions of the poets), is gained at the expense of a surrender of concrete thinking, at the expense of a generalization and an abstraction—which are arbitrary actions, decisions of the will, practical acts, and, as such, alien and hostile to the world of art.

4 [G. W. Leibniz, *Opera omnia,* ed. L. Dutens, II (Geneva: Tournes, 1768), 38.]

It so happens that art displays much more antagonism toward the positive and mathematical sciences than toward philosophy, religion, and history because the latter present themselves as fellow citizens in the same world of theory or knowledge, while the former offend it with their coarse practical attitude toward contemplation. Poetry and classification, and worse still, poetry and mathematics, seem to go as little together as fire and water. The *esprit mathématique* and the *esprit scientifique* are the most avowed enemies of the *esprit poétique*. The periods in which natural sciences and mathematics prevail (for example, the intellectualistic eighteenth century) are the most sterile in poetry.

This rehabilitation of the nonlogical character of art is, as I have said, the most difficult and important of the arguments implicit in the formula of art-as-intuition. For the theories which attempt to explain art as philosophy, as religion, as history, as science, and, to a lesser degree, as mathematics occupy in fact the greater part of the history of aesthetic science, and are adorned with the names of the greatest philosophers. In the philosophy of the nineteenth century, examples of the identification or confusion of art with religion and with philosophy are offered by Schelling[k] and Hegel[l]; of its confusion with the natural sciences, by Taine[m]; of its confusion with historical and documentary data, by the theories of the French verists; and of its confusion with mathematics, by the formalism of the Herbartians.[n] However, it would be vain to look into all these authors, and into others who might be mentioned, for pure instances of those errors because error is never "pure," since, if such were the case, it would be truth.

Accordingly, even the doctrines which for the sake of brevity I shall call the "conceptualistic" theories of art contain in themselves dissolvent elements. Such elements are all the more numerous and effective the more dynamic is the spirit of the philosopher who professed them; and for this reason nowhere else are they so numerous and effective as in Schelling and Hegel, who had such a vivid sense of artistic production as to suggest, with their observations and their particular elaborations, a theory opposite to that which is at the basis of their systems. Aside from this, the conceptualistic theories themselves are not only superior to those examined previously, to the extent that they recognize the *theoretical* character of art, but also they make their own contribution to the true doctrine, thanks to their demand for a determination of the relations between fancy and logic, art and thought—relations which, though they are of things distinct, involve unity too.

And here we may already see that the simplest of formulas, that "art is intuition," when translated into other words synonymous with it (for example, that "art is a product of fancy"), is heard straight from the mouths of all those who converse daily about art, and is recognizable under older terms ("imitation," "fiction," "fable," etc.) in so many ancient books. Presented as it now is, within the context of a philosophical discussion, the formula is replete with historical, critical, and polemical content, of whose richness we have been able to offer hardly a foretaste. Nor will it be any longer a surprise that the philosophical conquest of that formula has cost an excessively large amount of toil, because that conquest is like setting foot atop a small hill long contested in battle, and so has an altogether different significance as compared with its easy ascent by the carefree climber in peacetime, its conquest being not a mere resting point at the end of a walk, but the net result and symbol of an army's victory. The historian of aesthetics traces the steps of the fatiguing advance, in which (and here is another magic of thinking) the victor, instead of losing strength on account of the blows inflicted upon him by the adversary, acquires new strength from these very blows, and reaches the desired hill by pushing back the adversary, yet still accompanying him.

I cannot here mention except in passing the importance of the Aristotelian concept of mimesis (which arose in opposition to the Platonic condemnation of poetry), and the attempt made by the same philosopher to distinguish *poetry* from *history*—a concept not sufficiently developed, and perhaps not altogether mature in his mind, and, hence, for a long time misunderstood. Still, after many centuries, it was to become the point of departure for aesthetic thought in modern times. I will also mention in passing the ever-growing awareness of the difference between *logic* and *fancy*, *judgment* and *taste*, *intellect* and *genius* which came to life in the course of the seventeenth century, and the serious form which the contrast between *Poetry* and *Metaphysics* took in Vico's *Scienza Nuova*.[o] In this connection, let me mention too the scholastic construction of an *Aesthetica*—distinct from a *Logica*—as *gnoseologia inferior*[5] and *scientia cognitionis sensitivae*[6] in the work of Baumgarten,[p] who in other respects remained entangled in the difficulties of the conceptualistic view of art and whose work was not on a par with the goal he had set for himself; the criticism of Kant against Baumgarten and all the Leibnizians and Wolffians[q]—a criticism which made clear why intuition is intuition and not just a "confused concept"; romanticism, which through its artistic criticism and its historical contributions, perhaps more than through its systems, developed the new idea of art announced by Vico; and, finally, in Italy, the type of criticism inaugurated by Francesco De Sanctis, who against all utilitarianism, moralism, and conceptualism asserted the rights of art as pure *form*[r] (to employ his own term), that is, as pure intuition.

Only, doubt crops up at the foot of truth "like a shoot," as Father Dante's tercet[7] puts it—doubt being after all the thing that drives the intellect of man on "from peak to peak." The doctrine of art as intuition, fancy or form, now gives rise to a further problem (I have not said as yet a "final" problem), which is no longer one of opposition and distinction with respect to physics, hedonistics, ethics, and logic, but is internal to the field itself of images. To doubt whether an image is sufficient to define the character of art really involves the question of how to differentiate a genuine from a spurious image, thereby enriching the concept of image and of art. What function (one may ask) can a world of mere images, without philosophic, historical, religious, or scientific value, not to mention moral or hedonistic

5 ["Science of inferior knowledge."]
6 ["Science of sensory knowledge."]
7 [Dante, *La Divina Commedia, Il Paradiso,* IV, 130–132.]

value, have for the human spirit? Is there anything more vain than to dream with eyes open for a life requiring not only eyes but also an open mind and an active spirit? Pure images, imagine that! Anyhow, to nourish oneself on pure images has a name, not too respectable, called "to fancy," to which there is often added the epithet "idle," and which is considered something quite inconclusive and insipid. But could *this* really be art?

To be sure, we take delight now and then in reading some sensational adventure story where images follow one after another in the most diverse and haphazard fashion. However, we amuse ourselves with it during moments of weariness, when we are forced to kill time. But even then we keep perfectly in mind that such trash is not art. Cases like this have to do with a game or a pastime. On the other hand, if art were a game or a pastime, it would fall right back into the wide arms of the hedonistic theories—arms ever ready to welcome it. Now, it is a utilitarian or hedonistic need which impels us to loosen occasionally the bow of the mind and of the will, and to lie down all stretched out, letting images in our memory unravel one by one or fitting them together in the imagination in the queerest of ways, as in a sort of daydream, which we snap out of as soon as we finish resting. Sometimes we snap out of it precisely in order to turn our attention to the work of art itself, which is never produced by anyone who is loafing.

Therefore, either art is not pure intuition and the requirements set by the doctrines which we thought we had refuted above remain unsatisfied, and, consequently, our refutation itself of those theories becomes dubious, or else intuition cannot consist of a simple imagining.

To make the problem more exact or more difficult, it would be well to eliminate from it at once that part to which the answer is easy, and which I did not want to overlook, precisely because it often gets mixed and confused with the problem itself. In reality, intuition is production of an image. But it is not production of an incoherent accumulation of images obtained by reconjuring up ancient images, letting them succeed each other at will, or combining them in the same arbitrary fashion, such as joining the neck of a horse to the human head, as is done in a child's game. In order to express this distinction between intuition and fantasy, the olden poetics made use, especially, of the concept of *unity* and required that any artistic work produced be *simplex et unum;* or it utilized the allied concept of *unity in variety,* according to which the several images were to come to a focus and blend into a complex image. To meet the same need, the aesthetics of the nineteenth century worked out the distinction (which is found in not a few of its philosophers) between *fancy* (corresponding to the artistic faculty proper) and *imagination* (corresponding to the extra-artistic faculty). To collect, select, divide, and combine images presupposes within the spirit the production and the possession of the single images themselves. Fancy is a producer, whereas imagination is a parasite, fit for incidental occasions but incapable of begetting organization and life.

The deepest problem underlying the somewhat superficial formula in terms of which I presented it at first is, therefore: what function belongs properly to pure image in the life of the spirit? Or (what amounts to the same thing), how does pure image originate? Every gifted work of art gives birth to a large band of imitators who just copy it, cut it to pieces, combine it with something else, distort it mechanically; they symbolize imagination versus or against fancy. But what is the justification, or what is the genesis of the gifted work, which gets subjected afterward (sign of glory) to so much abuse? In order to clarify this point, it is still necessary to go deeper into the nature of fancy and pure intuition. The best way to undertake this deeper examination is to recall and criticize the theories through which an attempt has been made (with precautions taken against falling into realism or conceptualism) to differentiate artistic intuition from mere inarticulate imagination, to ascertain in what the principle of unity consists, and to justify the productive character of fancy.

The artistic image (it has been said) is such, when it attaches an intelligible to a sensible, and represents an *idea.* Now "intelligible" and "idea" cannot have any other meaning (nor have

they had any other for the defenders of this theory) than concept, even though it is the concrete concept or idea, which is
peculiar to lofty philosophical speculation and differs from
abstract concepts and from those representative of the sciences.
But, in any case, the concept or idea unites the intelligible with
the sensible in every instance, and not solely in art. For the new
conception of the concept, inaugurated by Kant and immanent
(so to speak) in all modern thought, heals the breach between
the sensible and the intelligible worlds, conceiving as it does
the concept as judgment, judgment as a priori synthesis, and a
priori synthesis as the word which becomes flesh, as history.
Thus, contrary to intention, that definition of art reduces fancy
to logic, and art to philosophy. At best, it proves effective against
the abstract conception of science, but not really as regards the
problem of art. (Incidentally, Kant's *Critique of Judgment*—
aesthetic and teleological—had precisely such historical function of correcting whatever of abstract still remained in the
Critique of Pure Reason.) To require a sensible element for the
concept, besides that one which it already possesses inherently
as concrete concept, and besides the words by means of which it
expresses itself, would be a superfluous thing. To be sure, if we
insist on this requirement, we avoid the conception of art as
philosophy or as history, but only to fall into the conception of
art as *allegory*.

The insurmountable difficulties of allegory are well known;
so is its barren and anti-artistic character known and universally
felt. Allegory is the extrinsic union, or the conventional and
arbitrary juxtaposition of two spiritual facts—a concept or
thought and an image—whereby it is posited that *this* image
must represent *that* concept. Moreover, not only does recourse
to allegory fail to explain the integral character of the artistic
image, but, what is more, it deliberately sets up a duality. For
given the juxtaposition of thought and image, thought remains
thought and image remains image, there being no relation between them. So much so that, whenever we contemplate the
image, we forget the concept without any loss, but, on the contrary, to our gain; and whenever we think the concept, we dis-

pel, likewise to our advantage, the superfluous and annoying image.

Allegory met with much favor in the Middle Ages, with its mixture of Germanic and Romanic elements, barbarism and culture, bold fancy and subtle reflection. However, this was owing to a theoretical prejudice, and not to the actual reality of medieval art itself, which, wherever it is art, ejects allegorism from itself or resolves it from within. This need to resolve allegoristic dualism leads, in fact, to refining the theory of intuition as allegory of the idea to the other theory, that of intuition as *symbol*. For in symbol the idea is no longer thinkable by itself, separable from the symbolizing representation, nor is the latter representable by itself effectively without the idea symbolized.

As Vischer [8] the aesthetician (upon whom must fall the blame, if upon anybody, for a comparison so prosaic regarding a subject so poetic and metaphysical) used to declare, the idea is all dissolved in the representation, just as a lump of sugar dissolved in a glass of water continues and functions in each molecule of water, yet is no longer recognizable as a lump of sugar. Only, the idea which has disappeared and has become all representation, the idea which it is not possible any longer to grasp as idea (except by extracting it, like sugar from sweetened water), is no longer idea. It is only the sign of the yet-to-be-discovered principle of the unity of the artistic image. Certainly, art is symbol, all symbol, that is, all significant. But symbol of what? Signifying what? Intuition is truly artistic, is truly intuition and not a chaotic accumulation of images, only when it has a vital principle which animates it and makes for its complete unity. But what is this principle?

The answer to such questions may be said to emerge as a result of the examination of what constitutes the greatest contrast of tendencies that has ever obtained in the field of art (and that does not appear exclusively during the period from which it gets its name and in which it was predominant): the contrast between *romanticism* and *classicism*. Defining in general terms, as is convenient to do here, and disregarding minor and accidental elements, romanticism requests of art, above all, a spontaneous and unrestrained outpouring of the passions—love and hate, anguish and joy, despair and elation. It readily contents itself with, and takes pleasure in, ethereal and indeterminate images, an uneven style and one making allusions to vague suggestions, indefinite phrases, striking and hazy outlines. In contrast, classicism adores the tranquil mind, the learned style, figures drawn according to their type and definite in their contours, and is fond of deliberation, balance, and clarity. Classicism has a decided tendency toward *representation,* while its counterpart has it toward *emotion.*

Whoever proceeds to take sides with one or the other point of view will find an abundance of reasons to defend it and refute the opposite point of view. For, the romantics ask: What good is an art full of neat images, if after all it does not speak to the heart? And if it does so speak, what difference does it make if the images are not nice and neat? But their opponents query: What good is all the flurry of the passions if the spirit does not end up with a beautiful image? On the other hand, if the image is beautiful and satisfies our taste, what difference does the absence of those emotions make, since everybody can get them outside of art anyway, and since life does not fail to furnish them in even greater number than is desirable at times?

But, when we start getting tired of the fruitless defense of one or the other partial point of view, when, above all, we turn away from the ordinary works of art, produced by the romantic and classical school, away from the works overflowing with passion and those tediously proper, and look at the works, not of the disciples, but of the masters, not of the mediocre, but of the greatest, the contrast is seen to disappear in the distance, there being no longer a way of making use of the motto of either school. The great artists, the great works of art, or the great portions of those works, cannot be called either romanticist or classicist, emotional or representative, because they are both classicist and romanticist, representations and feelings: a strong feeling, which has become the perfect representation throughout.

Such, in particular, are the works of Greek art; and those of

Italian art and poetry, where medieval transcendence becomes fixed in the bronze of the Dantesque tercet; melancholy and suave fancy, in the transparency of Petrarch's[t] sonnets and ballads; insight into life and ridicule of the fables of the past, in the lucid octave of Ariosto[u]; heroism and meditation on death, in the faultless blank-verse hendecasyllables of Foscolo[v]; the utter vanity of everything, in the sober and austere songs of Giacomo Leopardi.[w] And (to add parenthetically and without intending a comparison with the other examples just cited), even the voluptuous nuances and the animal sensuality of current and international decadentism have had perhaps their best expression in the prose and verse of an Italian, D'Annunzio.[x] All those poets were profoundly passionate souls (yes, including the serene Lodovico Ariosto—so loving, so tender, and frequently repressing emotion with a smile); and their works of art constitute the eternal flower which bursts forth from their passions.

These experiences and critical judgments may be condensed theoretically into the following statement: what lends coherence and unity to intuition is intense feeling. Intuition is truly such because it expresses an intense feeling, and can arise only when the latter is its source and basis. Not idea but intense feeling is what confers upon art the ethereal lightness of the symbol. Art is precisely a yearning kept within the bounds of a representation. In art the yearning [for expression] is there solely for the sake of the representation, and representation solely for the sake of the yearning. Epic and lyric, or drama and lyric, are scholastic divisions of the indivisible. Art is always lyrical, or, if you like, the epic and drama of feeling.

What we admire in genuine works of art is the perfect imaginative form that a state of mind assumes there; and this is called the life, unity, compactness, and fullness of the work of art. What displeases us in spurious and poor works of art is the unresolved conflict of many different states of mind—their stratification or mixture or vacillating manner—which acquires an apparent unity from the sheer will of the author, who for such purposes avails himself of some scheme or abstract idea or an extra-aesthetic outburst of the passions. Series of images, which separately seem to be rich in significance, leave us afterward disappointed and diffident, because we do not see them issue from a state of mind, from a "quick sketch" (as painters are accustomed to say), from a motif. They succeed each other and are bunched together without that proper intonation or accent which comes from within.

Now then, what is a figure in a picture when removed from its own background and placed against another one? What is a personage in a drama or novel outside of his relation with all the other personages and action in general? And what value does this action in general have if it is not an action of the spirit of the author? In this connection, instructive are the very old disputes concerning dramatic unity, which, starting from the external elements of time and place, was first carried over to the unity of "action," and this eventually to the unity of "interest," where the latter in its turn was to have culminated in the interest of the spirit of the poet, in the ideal which inspires him. Also instructive are, as we have seen, the critical results of the great debate between classicists and romanticists, wherein was denied both the art which, by appealing to feeling in the abstract, to virtual outbursts of feeling, to feeling not yet transformed into contemplation, tries to confuse minds and deceive them about its lack of imagery; as well as the art which, by appealing to superficial clarity, to misleadingly accurate drawings, to misleadingly exact words, attempts to cover up an absence of aesthetic reason to justify its figments, to cover up a lack of emotional inspiration.

A celebrated saying, which we owe to an English critic[y] and which is by this time found among journalistic commonplaces, declares that "All art [constantly] aspires towards the condition of music."[8] Concerning which it would be necessary to state more exactly that all the arts are music, if thereby we wish to give emphasis to the emotional origin of artistic images, excluding from their number those constructed mechanically or burdened with realism. And another, no less celebrated saying, which we

8 [Walter Pater, *The Renaissance* (London, Macmillan, 1900), p. 135. Croce omits in Italian the adverb "constantly" in the original.]

owe to a Swiss semiphilosopher,^z and which has been subject to the same good or bad fortune of becoming trivial, announces that "every landscape is a state of mind."[9] This is doubtless true, not because a landscape is a landscape, but because it is art.

Artistic intuition is, therefore, always *lyric* intuition. This word "lyric" is not being used here as an adjective or predicate of "intuition," but as a synonym—another of the synonyms which can be added to the several I have already mentioned, all of which denote intuition. And, if it is useful at times that "lyric" as synonym assume the grammatical form of the adjective, this is only in order to make intelligible the difference between true intuition and false intuition. That is to say, between, on the one hand, intuition-as-image or system of images (inasmuch as what is called image is always a system of images, there existing no images-in-isolation, any more than thoughts-in-isolation)—which constitutes a living system, and being such, possesses its own vital principle, namely, the living system itself —and, on the other hand, a conglomeration of images, put together for fun or business or for some other practical end, and whose system, being practical in nature, turns out to be, when considered from an aesthetic aspect, not really organic but mechanical. Yet, aside from this particular explanatory and polemical function, the term "lyric" is redundant, since art continues to be perfectly defined when defined simply as *intuition*.

[9] [Henri-Frédéric Amiel, *Fragments d'un journal intime,* 14th ed. (Paris, Fischbacher, 1922), p. 62.]

II. *Prejudices Concerning Art*

The elaboration of the distinction that I have traced, in summary fashion, between art and everything with which it has been, or is usually, confused, doubtless costs not a little mental effort. But this exertion somehow obtains its reward in the end in the form of the independence, which is acquired by its means, toward the many fallacious distinctions that encumber the field of aesthetics. These distinctions, though they may look attractive at first, on account of their very glibness and deceptive clarity actually interfere with all profound understanding of what art really is. And, although there is no shortage of those who, for the sheer convenience of repeating traditional and popular distinctions, resign themselves willingly to understanding nothing, it now behooves us, instead, to throw away all these distinctions (since they are obstacles to the new task to which the new theoretical orientation invites us and leads us), and so enjoy the greatest ease which comes from feeling rich. For wealth is acquired not solely through the possession of many goods, but also through the elimination of all those which are economic *liabilities*.

Let us begin with the most famous of these economic liabilities in the field of aesthetics: the distinction between *content* and *form*—a distinction which in the nineteenth century gave rise to a celebrated split in schools of aesthetics, to wit, the aesthetics of content (*Gehaltsaesthetik*) and the aesthetics of form (*Formaesthetik*).[a]

The problems from which those opposite schools of thought arose were, roughly, the following: Does art consist of content alone, or form alone, or of both form and content? What is the nature of content, the nature of aesthetic form? One group replied that art resides wholly in content, defined from time to time as whatever pleases, is moral, raises man to the empyrean of metaphysics and religion, is a fact, or, even, is naturally and physically beautiful. The other group said that content is immaterial, being simply a peg or frame on which to hang beautiful forms, and that these alone beautify the aesthetic spirit with their unity, harmony, symmetry, and the like. From one and the other camp an attempt was made to win over to its side, by means of subsumption, the element which had originally been excluded from the nature of art. The content-ists conceded that it behooved content (which was, according to them, the constitutive element of the beautiful) to adorn itself with beautiful forms too, and manifest itself with unity, symmetry, harmony, and so forth. The formalists, in their turn, conceded that, though art itself would not gain from the value of content, its effect would, since then we would have the benefit of not just one value alone, but that [accruing] from the sum of two values.

These doctrines, which attained their most voluminous academic expression in Germany among the Hegelians and the Herbartians, are to be found for one thing, to some extent, throughout the history of aesthetics—ancient, medieval, modern, and recent—and, what is of greater consequence, are to be found among popular opinions. For nothing is so common as to hear that a drama is beautiful in "form" but mistaken in "content"; that a poem is most noble "in conception" but "expressed in ugly verses"; that a painter would be greater if he did not waste his power as designer and colorist on "trivial and unworthy themes," but selected instead others of historical, patriotic, or sociological importance.

One may say that a fine taste and a genuine critical sense of art are obliged to defend themselves constantly against the distortions of judgment which emerge from these doctrines, where the philosophers become mob, and the mob almost feels philosopher, since it sees itself in agreement with those mob-philosophers. The origin of these doctrines is no secret to us because, even from the brief indication already given, it is clear that they sprout from the trunk of the hedonistic, moralistic, conceptualistic, or physical conceptions of art. Since these conceptions do not comprehend what makes art what it is, they are later constrained to recapture somehow the art which they had let escape by reintroducing it under the guise of an accessory or accidental element, with the content-ists conceiving it as the abstract element of form, the formalists as the abstract element of content.

What interests us about those aesthetic theories is precisely this very dialectic, through which the content-ists become involuntarily formalists, and the formalists, content-ists. One group lands in the other's position, only to feel restless there and turn back to its own—which provokes the same restlessness all over again. The "beautiful forms" of the Herbartians differ nowise from the "beautiful contents" of the Hegelians because the one and the other are *nothing*. And it is of even more interest to us to observe the efforts on the part of some of those thinkers to escape from prison, to watch how they weaken its doors and walls with their blows, and to take note of the holes that they, in effect, manage to open. Efforts awkward and sterile, like those of the content-ists (as evident, for example, in Hartmann's[b] *Philosophie des Schönen*), who, by knitting stitch by stitch and fashioning a net out of their beautiful "contents" (beautiful, sublime, comic, tragic, humoristic, pathetic, idyllic, sentimental, etc.), sought to have it embrace every form of reality including even the one that they had called "ugly." But they did not perceive that their aesthetic content, formulated little by little to coincide with the whole of reality, no longer had any trait which would distinguish it from other contents, there being no other content outside of reality. Which means that their fundamental theory came to be, thereby, fundamentally negated.

Tautologies, like those of other formalistic content-ists, who defended the concept of an aesthetic content, but defined it as "what is of human interest,"[c] taking interest as something relative to man under various historical situations, in other words, as relative to the individual. This was another way of denying the fundamental issue since it is quite clear that no artist would produce art if he did not interest himself in something which constitutes the datum or the problem of his production. But this something becomes art only because the artist, who has interested himself in it, has made it such. Subterfuges of formalists, who, after having restricted art to beautiful abstract forms, void in themselves of any content and yet capable of being joined to various contents (thus adding up to a sum, as it were, of two values), timidly introduced among the beautiful forms that of the "harmony of form with content." Or, more resolutely, they declared themselves partisans of a kind of eclecticism, which made art lie in the "relation" of a beautiful content with a beautiful form. And so, with the inaccuracy worthy of eclectics, they attributed to terms outside of the relation, qualities that they assume only within the relation.

For the truth is really this: content and form should be properly distinguished in art. However, neither one can separately qualify as artistic, precisely because their relation alone is artistic, that is, their unity, understood not as an abstract and lifeless unity, but that concrete and living one which constitutes the a priori synthesis. Art is a true *aesthetic a priori synthesis* of feeling and image within intuition. Of which it can be said anew that intense feeling without image is blind, and image without intense feeling is empty. Feeling and image, outside the aesthetic synthesis, do not exist for the artistic spirit. They could exist under different aspects in other domains of the spirit. Feeling would then be the practical aspect of the spirit, which loves and hates, desires and shuns; and image would be the inanimate residue of art, the withered leaf prey to the wind of the imagination and to amusement's whims.

Yet all this makes no difference either to the artist or to the aesthetician because art is not a vain indulging in fancies, nor is it a tumultuous passionateness, but the transcendence of this behavior thanks to another, or, if one so prefers, the replacement of this tumult with another type of tumult, possessing the yearning to create and contemplate, and the joys and sorrows of artistic creation. It is immaterial, therefore, or it is a matter of mere terminological convenience, to describe art as content or form, provided that it is always understood that content is given form and form is given content, that feeling is a feeling which is formed, and form is a form which is felt. And only out of respect

for the man who, better than others, vindicated the concept of
the autonomy of art, and who liked to do so by means of the
term "form," thereby opposing the abstract content-ism of the
would-be philosophers and moralists, as well as the abstract
formalism of the academicians—out of respect, I say, for De
Sanctis—and likewise owing to the ever-urgent need to coun-
teract attempts at absorbing art into other modes of spiritual
activity, the Aesthetics of intuition could be named "Aesthetics
of form."

There is no point to rebut with an objection, which could
certainly be raised (though more out of legal sophistry than
scientific acumen), namely, that even the Aesthetics of intuition,
in specifying the content of art as feeling or a state of mind, considers it as outside of intuition and thus seems to acknowledge
that a content which is not an intense feeling or a state of mind
does not lend itself to artistic elaboration and is not an aesthetic
content. But feeling or state of mind is not a particular content,
it is the whole universe viewed *sub specie intuitionis*[1]; and beyond it no other content is conceivable which is not at the same
time a form different from the intuitive one. Feelings are not
thoughts—which constitute the whole universe *sub specie cogi-
tationis*[2]; nor physical things and mathematical entities—which
constitute the whole universe *sub specie schematismi et abstrac-
tionis*[3]; nor volitions—which constitute the whole universe *sub
specie volitionis.*[4]

Another no less fallacious distinction (to which it is also
customary to assign the terms "content" and "form") separates
intuition from *expression,* image from its physical rendition. It
puts on one side impressions of feelings, images of men, animals,
landscapes, actions, adventures, etc., and on the other, sounds,
tones, lines, colors, etc. It calls the latter the external component
of art, the former the internal: one, *art* proper, and the other,
technique.[d] It is easy to distinguish here internal and external,
in words at least, especially when the mode of distinction and

1 ["From the intuitive aspect."]
2 ["From the intellectual aspect."]
3 ["From the schematic and abstract aspect."]
4 ["From the volitional aspect."]

the reasons for it are not examined closely, and when the distinction itself is abandoned later without requiring it to do anything. So easy that, without ever giving it another thought, the distinction can even seem indubitable to the understanding. However, it becomes a different matter when, as with every distinction, one turns from the business of distinguishing things to that of setting up their relationship and mode of bringing them together, because then we run up against most hopeless obstacles.

The distinction in question, having been poorly made to begin with, cannot be unified again. How can something external, or alien to the internal, be joined with the internal and express it? How can a sound or a color express a soundless and colorless image? Or a body express the bodiless? How can fancy (with its spontaneity) and reflection (or better still, technical activity) belong to the same act? Once intuition is distinguished from expression, with the nature of one made different from the nature of the other, no amount of ingenuity in the use of middle terms can ever succeed in soldering them together. All the processes of association, habit, mechanization, forgetfulness, instinctive behavior, which psychologists have proposed and laboriously developed, end up with the reappearance of the gap, with expression at one corner and image at the other. And it seems that there is no other way out to take refuge in the hypothesis of a mystery, which, according to tastes now poetical, now mathematical, will be represented as a mysterious matrimony or as a mysterious psychophysical parallelism, where the former in its turn is a parallelism surmounted spuriously, and the latter, a matrimony celebrated ages and ages ago or in the darkness of the unknowable. But before having recourse to mystery (which is a refuge there is always time for), it is necessary to find out whether the two elements have been legitimately distinguished, and whether an intuition without expression exists or is conceivable. Perhaps the whole thing is as inexistent and inconceivable as a soul without a body—regarding which, to tell the truth, there has been much talk among philosophies no less than among religions, yet this in itself does not signify having experienced it and conceived such.

In reality, we do not know anything but intuitions that are

expressed. A thought is not for us thought unless it is formulated into words. Neither is a musical fancy unless it is made concrete through sounds, nor a pictorial imagination unless it is rendered in color. We are not saying that the words must necessarily be spoken aloud, the music performed, or the painting depicted on canvas or wood. However, it is certain that when a thought is truly such, when it has reached its maturity, words circulate throughout our whole organism, stimulating the muscles of our mouth and resounding internally in our ear. When a piece of music is truly music, it trills in the throat or trembles in the fingers that run up and down ideal keyboards. When a pictorial image is really such, we are pregnant with lymphs that are colors, and it may well be the case that, were coloring materials not at our disposal, we would spontaneously color surrounding objects by means of a sort of irradiation, as is reported of certain hysterical individuals and saints who used to impress stigmata upon their hands and feet with the help of imagination!

Prior to the formation of this expressive state of the spirit, not only were thought, musical fancy, pictorial image inexistent without their expressions, they did not exist at all. It is naïve to believe in their pre-existence—if it is naïve to give credit to those impotent poets, painters, or musicians who always have their heads filled with poetic, pictorial, and musical creations, and yet do not succeed in translating them into external form, either because, as they say, they are intolerant to expression or because technique has not progressed far enough to provide sufficient means for their expression. Many centuries ago, technique was adequate enough for Homer, Phidias,[e] or Apelles,[f] but not for them, who, according to their own utterances, carry a greater art in their huge heads! Sometimes that naïve belief originates from an illusion due to an overestimation of ourselves. The illusion arises whenever, just because we have conceived and, as a consequence, expressed a few individual images, we fancy that we already have in our possession all the rest of the images which are to go into a work (but which we do not as yet possess), as well as the vital link which is to join them together, but which has not come into existence as yet. This explains why neither the one (the images) nor the other (their link) has been given expression.

Art understood as intuition (in accordance with the concept which I have expounded), having denied a physical world facing it and having considered that world as an abstract construction of our intellect, does not know what use to make of the parallelism of thinking substance and extended substance. There is no need for art to promote impossible marriages because its thinking substance or, to be more exact, its intuitive activity is complete in itself and constitutes that very same fact which the intellect constructs later as extended. And to the extent that an image without expression is inconceivable, so an image that is at the same time expression, that is, really image, is conceivable, indeed logically necessary. If the meter, rhythm, and words of a poem are taken away from it, there does not remain beyond them all, as some suppose, its poetic thought. There remains nothing. The poem is born as those words, that rhythm, and that meter. Expression could not even be compared to the epidermis of an organism, unless it be said (and perhaps it would not even be false to say so in physiology) that the entire organism, in each of its cells and in each cell's cell, is epidermis throughout.

Still, I would be falling short of my methodological convictions as well as of the goal of rendering justice to errors (I have already done justice to the duality of content and form by showing the truth toward which it was tending, but which it failed to attain) if I did not indicate likewise what truth lies at the bottom of this attempt to distinguish that indistinguishable called intuition into intuition and expression. Fancy and technique are distinguishable for good reason (though not as elements of art), and they are bound up and related with each other, though not in the field of art but in that vaster realm of the spirit in its totality. Technical or practical problems to solve, difficulties to overcome doubtless confront the artist, and there is really something which, even though not "physical" but spiritual (as everything real must be), can with respect to intuition be considered metaphorically as physical. What is this something?

The artist, whom we have left vibrating with expressive images that break forth from his entire being via infinite channels, is a whole man, and, hence, a practical man too. As such, he instructs the media of art not to allow the results of his spiritual labor to go to waste, and so make possible and facilitate, for himself and others, the *reproduction* of his images. Wherefore he devotes himself to practical activities which are at the service of that work of reproduction. These practical activities are, as every practical act, under the guidance of cognitions, and are said to be technical for this reason. Being practical and different from intuition—which is theoretical—such activities appear external to the latter, and are, therefore, called physical. They acquire this name all the more easily because they are fixed and abstracted by the intellect. Thus, writing and phonographs become associated with words and music; canvases, panels, and walls having coats of colors, with painting; stones carved, iron and bronze and other metals smelted, hammered, and wrought into various shapes, with sculpture and architecture.

So clearly are the two forms of activity distinguishable from each other that one could be a great artist but a poor technician; a poet who does a poor job of correcting the galley proofs of his own verses; an architect who makes use of unsuitable materials and fails to take statics sufficiently into account; a painter who uses colors which change rapidly. Examples of these shortcomings are so common that it is not worth while to cite them. But what is impossible is to be a great poet who writes poor verses, a great painter who does not know how to match colors, a great architect who does not know how to harmonize lines, a great musician who does not know how to bring tones into harmony—in short, a great artist who does not know how to express himself. It has been said of Raphael that he would have been a great painter even had he not had hands; but certainly not that he would have been a great painter even if he had lacked a sense of design.

Moreover (let it be noted in passing, as I must proceed in concise fashion), this apparent transformation of intuitions into physical things—exactly analogous to the apparent transformation of needs and economic work into things and goods—also explains how it comes about that we talk not only of "artistic things" and "beautiful things" but even of a "beauty of nature."ᵍ It is evident that, besides the instruments which are devised for the reproduction of images, one can also find objects already in existence (whether products of man or no) which accomplish the same task, that is, are more or less suitable to preserve the memory of our intuitions. These things assume the name of "natural beauties" and exercise their power only when one knows how to see them with the same perspective from which they have been seen and are appropriated by the artist or the artists who have exploited them and established the "point of view" from which they are to be beheld, thereby connecting them with an intuition of theirs. But the ever-imperfect suitability, transiency, and variability of "natural beauties" also justify the inferior place assigned to them when they are compared with the beauties produced by art. We leave to the rhetoricians and the exuberant to affirm that a beautiful tree, a grand river, a majestic mountain, or even a beautiful horse or a beautiful human figure are superior to the chisel strokes of Michelangelo or the verses of Dante. As for us, we declare, with greater appropriateness, that "nature" is stupid compared to art, and that she is "dumb," if man does not make her speak.

A third distinction, which also strives hard to distinguish the indistinguishable, adheres to the concept of aesthetic expression, dividing it into two types: expression in the strict sense (expression *proper*) and beauty of expression (*ornate* expression). Upon these two rests the classification of two orders of expression, simple and ornate expressions. This is a doctrine, traces of which can be discovered in all the various domains of art, but which has not been so highly developed in any of them as in the domain of words where it goes under a famous name, "Rhetoric." The doctrine has gone through a very long history, from the Greek rhetoricians down to our own day, and continues to exist in schools, treatises, and even in aesthetic theories with scientific pretensions, as well as (which is natural) in popular opinion, although at the present moment it has lost much of its original vigor.[h] Men of great intelligence, by dint of inertia or tradition, have for centuries accepted it or allowed it to live. Its few rebels have hardly ever attempted to reduce their rebellion to systematic form and to remove the error at its roots.

The harm done by Rhetoric, with its idea that "ornate" speech is different from and more precious than "simple" speech, has not been restricted to the field of aesthetics alone, but has spilled over into the field of criticism and even frequently into literary education. For the more Rhetoric was unable to justify pure beauty, the more was it suited to offer an apparent justification of artificial beauty, and to encourage writing in high-flown, affected, and improper form. However, the division Rhetoric introduces and on which it rests, contradicts itself logically because, as it is easy to prove, it destroys the concept itself of expression (which it tries to divide into types) and the objects of expression (which it attempts to divide into classes). A proper expression, if proper, is also beautiful—beauty being nothing but the determination of the image, and, hence, of the expression. Now, if by calling it simple one wishes to warn that something is missing in it which should be there, in that case it is improper or deficient, that is, it is not expression, or not as yet so. Conversely, an ornate expression, if it is expressive in every part, cannot be said to be ornate, but as simple and as proper as its counterpart. If it contains inexpressive, superfluous, extrinsic elements, it is not beautiful but ugly, that is to say, it is not expressive, or not as yet so. For this reason it must purify itself of extraneous elements, as its counterpart must enrich itself with the elements missing.

Expression and beauty are not two concepts, but a single concept, which may be designated with either of the synonymous terms. Artistic fancy has always a corporeal frame but not corpulence; it is always dressed properly, yet never overdressed or "ornate." To be sure, under this falsest of distinctions there was brooding a problem too; hence, the need for making some distinction. The problem (as may be inferred from somewhere in

Aristotle, from the psychology and epistemology of the Stoics, and as it appears more clearly in the discussions of the Italian rhetoricians of the seventeenth century) had to do with the relations between thought and fancy, philosophy and poetry, logic and aesthetics (between "dialectic" and "rhetoric," or the "closed fist" and the "open hand,"[1] as it used to be said then). "Simple" expression was an allusion to thought and philosophy, and "ornate" expression to fancy and poetry. Still, it is no less true that this problem of the distinction between the two forms of the theoretical spirit could not be solved in the field of one of them alone—that of intuition or expression—where nothing else will ever be found except fancy, poetry, and aesthetics. The illegitimate introduction of logic will only cast there a deceptive shadow which will obfuscate and obstruct intelligence, preventing it from beholding art in its fullness and purity, without affording it that view belonging to logic and thought.

However, the gravest harm that the rhetorical doctrine of "ornate" expression has brought to the theoretical systematization of the forms of the human spirit concerns the treatment of language. For, when simple and purely grammatical expressions as well as ornate or rhetorical expressions are taken for granted, language becomes necessarily attached to simple expressions and relegated to grammar, and ultimately (since grammar finds no place in rhetoric and aesthetics) to logic, where the subordinate function of a semiotic or *ars significandi*[5] is assigned to it. In fact, the logicist conception of language is closely connected and proceeds at equal pace with the rhetorical theory of expression. They were born together in ancient Greece and still live together, though in opposition, in our own times.

The revolts against logicism in theory of language have been as rare and have had as little effect as those against rhetoric. Only in the romantic period (anticipated by Vico a century before) did there develop, among certain thinkers or among certain circles, a vivid awareness of the *imaginative* or *metaphorical* nature of language and of its closer tie to poetry than to logic.

[5] ["Theory of signs."]

Nevertheless, even among the best of the thinkers, there persisted a very strong resistance to the *identification of language and poetry,* owing to the prevalence of a more or less extra-artistic notion of art (conceptualism, moralism, hedonism, etc.). Yet, now that we have established the concept of art as intuition and of intuition as expression and, therefore, by implication, the identity of the latter with language, the above identification appears to us as unavoidable as obvious, provided, of course, that language is taken in its whole extension (that is, without arbitrarily limiting it to so-called articulate language, or without arbitrarily excluding its tonal, imitative, or graphic forms) and in its whole intension, that is, taken in its reality as the act itself of speech, without falsifying it with the abstractions of grammars and dictionaries, and without imagining foolishly that man speaks out of a dictionary or a grammar.

Man speaks at every instant like the poet because, like the poet, he expresses his impressions and his feelings in the form called ordinary conversation. Ordinary conversation is not separated by any abyss from other forms named prosaic, poetic prose, narrative, epic, dialogue, dramatic, lyric, melodic, singing, and so forth. If man in general is not displeased with being considered a poet now and always (as he is by virtue of his humanity) it should not displease a poet to join hands with the common man because this union alone explains the power that poetry, understood in the strict and sublime sense, exerts over all human minds. Were poetry a tongue apart, a "language of the gods,"[j] men would not understand it. If it ennobles them, it does so not from above but from within themselves. The true democracy and the true aristocracy, even in this case, coincide.

Coincidence of art and language signifies, naturally, coincidence of Aesthetics and Philosophy of language, each definable in terms of the other, the two being identical. This is what I ventured to convey several years ago via the title of a treatise of mine on aesthetics,[k] which has not failed to have its effect upon many linguists as well as philosophers of art, inside and outside Italy, as is evident from the copious "literature" that has arisen around it. This identification will bring benefit to studies of art and poetry by purifying them of hedonistic, moralistic, and conceptualistic residues which are still so noticeable in literary and artistic criticism. But no less considerable will be the benefit that will accrue to linguistic studies, which badly need to be disencumbered from the physiological, psychological, and psychophysiological methods now in vogue and emancipated from the ever-recurring theory of the *conventional* origin of language which carries with it, as an inevitable reaction, its inevitable correlate of the *mystical* theory. It will no longer be necessary, even here, to construct absurd parallelisms or advocate mysterious marriages between image and sign, inasmuch as language is no longer conceived as sign, but as image which is significant, in other words, as its own sign, and, hence, colored, sonorous, or singing. Significant image is the spontaneous work of fancy, whereas signs, by means of which men come to terms with each other, presuppose image and, therefore, language. When we insist on explaining speech through the concept of sign, we are obliged in the end to resort to a God as donor of original signs, that is, to presuppose another conception of language, pushing it back to the unknowable.

I will close my account of the prejudices regarding art with the one which is most utilized because it is intermixed with the daily life of criticism and of art history: the preconception as to the possibility of distinguishing several or many *special forms of art,* each determinable in its specific concept and within its limits, and each furnished with its own laws.

This erroneous doctrine develops in two systematic series.[1] One of them is known as *theory of literary and artistic genres* (lyric, drama, novel, epic and romantic poetry, idyl, comedy, and tragedy; sacred painting, painting of civil and domestic life, painting from life, still life, landscape painting, flower and fruit painting; heroic, funerary, and ornamental sculpture; chamber, church, and operatic music; civil, military, and religious architecture; etc., etc.). The other is known as *theory of the arts* (poetry, painting, sculpture, architecture, music, the art of acting, of gardening, etc., etc.). At times one of these theories functions as a subdivision of the other.

Even this preconception, whose origin is easy to understand anyway, acquires its first distinguished pillars in Greek culture, and it likewise continues to exist at present. Many aestheticians still write treatises on the aesthetics of the tragic, the comic, the lyric, or the humorous, and on the aesthetics of painting, music, or poetry (these last going under the old name of Poetics). But what is worse (since those aestheticians are but little heeded and write for their private enjoyment or out of academic necessity), critics in judging works of art have not altogether given up the habit of measuring them against the *genre* or the *particular art* to which, according to them, they should be assigned. Instead of making clear whether a work is beautiful or ugly, they proceed to rationalize their impressions by stating that it properly observes (or improperly violates) the rules of drama, novel, painting, or low relief.

Besides, quite widespread is the custom of treating artistic and literary histories as *histories of genres,* and of presenting artists as cultivators of this or that genre. An artist's work, which always possesses unity in its development, no matter whether the form it takes be lyric, novel, or drama, is broken up into as many little compartments as there are genres. Thus, for example, Lodovico Ariosto at one time appears among the cultivators of Latin poetry in the Renaissance, another time among the vernacular lyricists, a third time among the authors of the first Italian satires, a fourth among the authors of the first comedies, and a fifth among the perfecters of the chivalric poem. As if Latin and vernacular poetry, satire and comedy and chivalric poem were not in fact the same poet Ariosto revealing the logic of his spiritual development in various attempts and under various forms!

This does not mean that the theory of the genres and of the arts has not had and does not have its inner dialectic and self-criticism, or its irony, depending on what we prefer to call it. Nobody ignores the fact that literary history is filled with cases of an established genre which the gifted artist disregards in his work, thereby arousing the wrath of the critics. However, their wrath fails to squelch the admiration and popularity of the work, with the net result that, since we are unable to blame the artist and are unwilling to blame the genres type of critic, we usually end up with a compromise. The genre is widened or a new one is welcomed next to it as a legitimized bastard. And the compromise lasts out of inertia until a new work of genius comes to overturn once more the fixed standard.

An irony of the doctrine is, in addition, the impossibility in which its theorists find themselves, of delimiting logically the genres and the arts. All the definitions elaborated by them, on being examined somewhat closer, either evaporate into the general definition of art or appear as an arbitrary raising of single works of art to the status of genre and norm, and as a consequence are not reducible to rigorous logical terms. And to what absurdities may the effort lead to determine rigorously what is indeterminable on account of the contradictoriness of the undertaking is discernible even among the greats, including Lessing,[m] who arrived at the silly notion that painting represents "bodies"—bodies, not actions and souls, and not the soul and action of the painter! Absurdities can also be seen in the questions that logically arise from that illogicalness. That is, once a determinate field is assigned to every genre and to every art, which genre or which art is *superior?* Is painting superior to sculpture, drama to lyric? Furthermore, once the powers of each art are recognized with the divisions in question, would it not be desirable to *reunite* the separate powers into a genre of art which will annihilate the others, as a coalition of armies does a single army? For example, does not an opera, where poetry, music, scenery, and decoration are reunited, display greater aesthetic power than a simple *Lied* of Goethe's or a drawing of Leonardo's?

Questions, distinctions, definitions, and judgments that elicit the revolt of the artistic and poetic sense, which loves each work for itself, for what it is—a living, individual and incomparable creature—and knows that every work has its own particular law and its full and irreplaceable value. This is why a conflict has arisen between the affirmative judgment of artistic souls and the negative judgment of professional critics, and between the affirmations of the latter and the negations of the former. Professional critics, rightly, pass for pedants at times, even though artistic souls in their turn are "disarmed prophets," that is, they are incapable of reasoning and deducing the correct theory immanent in their judgments, and of setting it against the pedantic theory of their foes.

The correct theory is precisely an aspect of the conception of art as intuition or lyrical intuition. Inasmuch as every work of art expresses a state of mind, and inasmuch as a state of mind is individual and always new, intuition implies infinite intuitions, which it is impossible to fit into a set of pigeonholes for genres, unless the set itself is composed, too, of infinite pigeonholes, and, thus, no longer pigeonholes for genres, but for intuitions. And, on the other hand, since the individuality of intuition implies the individuality of expression, and since a painting is different from another painting no less than from a poem, and since painting and poetry are not valuable on account of the sounds vibrating in the air or because of the colors refracted from light, but owing to what they know how to convey to the spirit insofar as they become part and parcel of it, it is vain to resort to abstract means of expression in order to set up another series of genera or classes. In fine, any theory whatever of the division of the *arts* is without foundation.

The genus or class is, in this case, one only—art itself or intuition—whereas particular works of art are actually infinite. All are original, each one untranslatable into the other (since to translate, to translate with artistry, is to create a new work of art), each one untamed by the intellect. Philosophically, no intermediate interposes itself between the universal and the particular, no series of genera or species, of *generalia*. Neither the artist who produces art, nor the spectator who contemplates it, has need of anything but the universal and the individual, or, better still, the universal individualized: the universal artistic activity, which is all epitomized and concentrated in the representation of a single state of mind.

Nevertheless, though the pure artist and the pure critic, as well as the pure philosopher, do not sympathize with *generalia*, genera or classes, the latter retain their utility in other respects. This utility is the true side (which I shall not let go unnoticed) of those erroneous theories. It is certainly profitable to weave a net out of *generalia,* not for the production of art (which is spontaneous), nor for its understanding (which is philosophical), but in order to amass and limit in some way or other the infinite number of individual intuitions for concentration and memory purposes, and in order to count somehow the countless number of single works of art. These classes, as is natural, are always to be handled according to either the image or the expression abstracted, and, therefore, as classes of states of mind (literary and artistic genres) and as classes of expressive media (the arts). There is no use here to object that the various genres and arts are differentiated arbitrarily and that the general dichotomy is itself arbitrary. For we concede, of course, that the whole procedure is arbitrary. However, its arbitrariness becomes subsequently innocuous and useful, owing to the very fact that the procedure itself has been shorn of every pretense at being a philosophical principle and a criterion for understanding art.

The various genres or classes facilitate the knowledge of art and art education, offering to the first a sort of index of the most important works of art, to the second a compendium of the most timely tips suggested by the practice of art. Everything depends on not confusing the indexes with reality, precepts or hypothetical imperatives with categorical imperatives—confusion easy to fall into, but one which should and can be avoided. First of all, books on literary principles, on rhetoric, and on grammar (with their divisions according to parts of speech and with their rules of morphology and syntax), on the art of musical composition, on metrics, on painting, and so forth, consist chiefly of indexes and sets of precepts. In the second place, in them are manifested tendencies toward particular expressions of art, in which case they are to be considered as art still in the abstract, in the making (the poetry of classicism and romanticism, purist or popularized grammars, etc.). Finally, in the third place, the books reveal efforts and attempts at a philosophical comprehension of their subject matter, but vitiated by the error already criticized of the divisions of the genres and the arts. Which error in due course, because of its contradictions, paves the way to the true doctrine of the individuality of art.

This doctrine, to be sure, produces a sort of dismay at first. Individual, original, untranslatable, unclassifiable intuitions seem to evade the dominion of thought, which could never master them except by relating them with each other. But this seems in fact to be prohibited by the doctrine we have elaborated, since it looks absolutely anarchist or near-anarchist, rather than liberal and tolerant. A short poem is aesthetically equal to a long poem; a tiny little picture or sketch, to an altar picture or a fresco. A letter may be no less artistic than a novel. Even a beautiful translation is as original as an original work! Could not these propositions be irrefutable because they are deduced logically from sound premises? Could not they be true, though paradoxical (and this is no doubt a merit), that is to say, opposed to common opinion? Still, could not they also perchance be in need of some supplement? There ought to be a way of ordering, subordinating, connecting, understanding, and mastering the reel of intuitions, if we do not want to get dizzy with them.

There is in fact such a way, and, in denying theoretical import to abstract classifications, it was not our intention to deny it to that genetic and concrete classification (which is not really "classification") called *history*. In history each work of art occupies the place which properly belongs to it, that one and no other. [To illustrate with Italian writers, take] the short ballad of Guido Cavalcanti[n] and the sonnet of Cecco Angiolieri,[o] which seem to be the sigh or the laugh of the instant; Dante's *Commedia*, which seems to foreshorten a millenium of the human spirit; Merlin Cocaio's[p] *Maccheronee*, which in the course of all the buffoonery unfolds into the finesse of poetry; and the sixteenth-century adaptation of the *Eneide* by Annibal Caro,[q] the terse prose of Sarpi,[r] or the florid and Jesuitical prose of Daniello Bartoli.[s] Thus, there is no need to judge a work as unoriginal when it is original by virtue of its having life; as small, when it is neither small nor large, being something not subject to measurement. Now, if you so wish, a work could be said to be small or large—but in a metaphorical sense—in order to make manifest certain preferences and to establish certain relations (other than arithmetical or geometrical) of importance. And it is in history, which is becoming ever richer and clearer (and certainly not in the pyramids of empirical concepts, which become more and more empty the more they soar and the sharper they get), that we find the link of all works of art or of all intuitions. For in history these appear organically connected as successive and necessary stages in the development of the spirit, each one a melody of the eternal poem which brings all the separate poems into harmony with itself.

III. *The Place of Art in the Spirit and in Human Society*

The dispute over the dependence or independence of art reached its climax during the romantic period when the motto "art for art's sake" was coined, and—in apparent antithesis—its counterpart, "art for life's sake." Even at that time, to tell the truth, the dispute was carried on more by literary men and artists than by philosophers. In our own time, interest in it has waned, dropping to a theme over which beginners amuse themselves and do their exercises, and to a subject for academic speeches. Yet, even before the romantic period, in fact, throughout the most ancient writings containing reflections on art, traces of it may be observed. And the very philosophers of aesthetics, even when it appears that they ignore the dispute (and they certainly scorn it in that vulgar form), actually do take it into consideration, and indeed one may say that they think of nothing else. For, to discuss the independence or dependence of art—its autonomy or heteronomy—signifies, at bottom, to inquire as to whether *art exists or does not,* and if it does, as to *what it is.*

An activity whose principle depends upon that of another is, substantially, this other activity, retaining for itself an existence purely hypothetical or conventional. Art which depends upon morals, pleasure, or philosophy is morals, pleasure, or philosophy, but not art. If art is not taken to be dependent but independent, it is fitting to investigate upon what its independence is grounded, that is to say, how art may be distinguished from morals, pleasure, philosophy, and all other things. This means to investigate the nature of art, and to posit whatever be its nature as truly autonomous. Furthermore, it may well be that those very persons who affirm the autonomous nature of art,

48

then assert that art, while having its own nature intact, is subordinate to another order of superior dignity, serving (as it used to be said at one time) as handmaiden to ethics, minister to politics, and interpreter to science. But this would only prove that there are people who have the habit of contradicting themselves or of thinking inconsistently—confused people whose life has really no need for proof at all. For our part, we will try not to fall into such confusion. Having already explained that art is distinguished from the so-called physical world as *spirituality,* and from practical, moral, and conceptual activity as *intuition,* we will not trouble ourselves any further and will assume that, with that prior proof, we have at the same time proved the *independence* of art. Still, implicit in the dependence-independence dispute is another problem which I have deliberately not discussed hitherto and which I will proceed to examine now.

Independence is a relational concept and, accordingly, there is nothing absolutely independent except the Absolute, or rather, except absolute relation. Every particular form or concept is independent in one respect and dependent in another, that is, independent and dependent simultaneously. If this were not so, spirit and reality in general would be either a series of juxtaposed absolutes, or (what amounts to the same thing) a series of juxtaposed nothings. The independence of a form presupposes the material with which it works, as we have already seen in elaborating upon the genesis of art as the intuitive organization of an emotional or passional material. Now, under a condition of absolute independence without any material to feed on, form itself, being empty, would nullify itself. But, since the acknowledged independence denies the possibility of considering one activity as subordinate to the principle of another, the dependence must be such as to guarantee independence. This would not even be guaranteed by the hypothesis of the mutual dependence of the two activities, conceived as two counteracting forces that cannot exceed each other. For if one of them were unable to exceed the other, there would be reciprocal interruption or neutralization, and, if it could, there would be dependence pure and simple—which has already been excluded. Therefore, considering the matter as a whole, it appears that there is no other mode of conceiving simultaneously the independence and dependence of the various spiritual activities except within the condition-conditioned relation, in which the conditioned transcends the condition it presupposes and then becomes in its turn condition for a new conditioned, thereby constituting a series in *development*.

There would be no other defect to impute to this series, except that its first term is a condition without a prior conditioned, and its last a conditioned which does not in its turn become condition—thus signifying a double violation of the law itself of development. Even this defect, however, gets remedied if the last is made the condition of the first and the first is made the conditioned of the last, in other words, if the series is conceived in the form of reciprocal action, or, to be more exact (and to abandon all naturalistic phraseology), is conceived as a *circle*. This conception seems to be the only way out of the difficulties in which the other conceptions of the spiritual life flounder, including both the one which makes it consist of a collection of independent and unrelated faculties of the soul, or of independent and unrelated ideas of value; as well as the other, which subordinates all the various faculties or ideas of value to one alone, resolving them therein into something which remains immobile and impotent, or, with more finesse, conceives them as necessary stages of a linear development, advancing from an irrational initial stage to a final stage which purports to be entirely rational, but which turns out to be really suprarational and, as such, also irrational itself.

However, as it would be advisable not to insist on this somewhat abstract scheme, let us rather consider how it gets incorporated into the life of the spirit beginning with the aesthetic spirit. With this in mind, let us return once more to the artist, or to man *qua* artist, who has brought to completion the process of liberation from emotional excitement, objectifying it in a lyrical image—in other words, has achieved art. In this image he finds his satisfaction because he has worked toward it, and has been moved. All know, to some degree, the joy of the perfect expression which we may succeed in giving to our own impulses, as well as the joy of successful expression of others' impulses (which are ours too) contemplated in their works— works which are in a certain sense ours, and which we make our own. Yet, is the satisfaction complete? Was man *qua* artist driven toward image alone? Toward *image* and toward *something else* at the same time. Toward image insofar as man is artist, and toward something else insofar as artist is man: toward image at the first level [of the process]. But, since the first level is connected with the second and third levels, he was also driven toward the latter two, although immediately toward the first, while mediately toward the second and third. Now that the first level has been reached, the second emerges right behind it, and from something aimed at indirectly becomes something of direct concern. And so a new requirement presents itself, and a new process is initiated.

I do not mean, let us bear carefully in mind, that the faculty of intuition should yield its place to another power, as if it were by turns at the other's pleasure or service; but rather, that the faculty of intuition, or better still, spirit itself, which at first appeared to be, and in a certain sense was, intuition in its entirety, develops within itself the new process which issues from the bowels of the old one. To avail myself again at this time of Dante's language, within us there is no kindling of "one soul above another." But the one soul, which at first is all concentrated within a single "faculty" and which "seems to heed no other power of hers" (being satisfied with that sole faculty— artistic imagery), comes to find within that faculty, not only her satisfaction, but her dissatisfaction too. Her satisfaction because it offers the soul all that it can offer and is expected of it; her dissatisfaction because, in spite of her having obtained all that and having her appetite satisfied to the full with its finest nectar, she "returns thanks for that, but asks for this."[1] That is, the soul requests satisfaction of her new appetite which

[1] [Dante, *La Divina Commedia, Il Purgatorio,* IV, 6; *ibid.,* 4; *Il Paradiso,* III, 93.]

has been brought about by the first satisfaction and which, without that initial satisfaction, could not have arisen.

In addition, we all recognize from constant experience the new want ensuing the formation of images. Ugo Foscolo has a love affair with Countess Arese. What that love is and who that woman is he does not ignore, as can be documented from the letters which he wrote to her and which may be read in print.[a] Yet, during the moments when he loves her that woman is his universe, and he feels his possession of her as the highest blessing; and, under admiration's spell, he aspires to change her as mortal into immortal, to transfigure her from something earthly into something divine for the faith of future generations, and to perform a new miracle through love's power. Indeed, he sees her taken up into heaven—an object of worship and prayer:

> And thou, divine one, shalt inherit through my hymns,
> The vows of the descendants of the Insubrians.[2]

Unless this metamorphosis of love had, for an instant, been entertained and desired with the greatest seriousness (lovers, and even the philosophers, if they have been in love at some time, can testify that these foolishnesses are taken seriously), the ode *All'amica risanata*[3] would not have attained form in Foscolo's mind. Furthermore, the images with which he represents the charm (so fraught with perils) of his goddess-mistress would not have been so vivid and spontaneous as they are. But, this impetus of spirit which has become now a magnificent lyrical representation, what was it? Was the subject—Foscolo the soldier, the patriot, the man of learning, the man stirred by so many spiritual needs—really exhausted in that yearning? Did not this yearning, in fact, operate so powerfully within him as to convert itself into action, and in some way serve as a guide to his practical life?

As Foscolo during the course of his love affairs had not lacked

[2] [Ugo Foscolo, *All'amica risanata*, last two lines of the ode. Original in Foscolo's *Opere edite e postume*, IX (Florence: Felice Le Monnier, 1923), 170.]

[3] ["To the Recuperated Friend."]

insight from time to time, so, in the presence of his poetry, with his creative outburst assuaged, he turns within himself and, on regaining or acquiring full clearness of vision, he asks himself and tries to establish what he really wanted and what that woman deserved. Perhaps an element of skepticism had already crept within him during the formation of the image, if our ears be not deceived in detecting, here and there, in the ode itself a certain undertone of elegant irony toward the woman and, on the part of the poet, toward himself. This is something that would not have happened to a more naïve spirit, inasmuch as the poetry itself then would have turned out to be quite naïve also. In any event, Foscolo as full-fledged poet and, for this reason, no longer poet (except to reappear as poet), now feels the need of knowing his actual situation. He no longer gives form to the image because he has already done so. Nor does he fancy, but perceives and reports: "that woman" (as he was to say of the "divine one" later) "had a piece of the brain where the heart is supposed to be."[b] Thus, the lyrical image is changed, for him and for us, into an item of autobiography, or into a *perception.*[c]

With *perception* we enter into a new and very vast field of the spirit. In truth, words are lacking to satirize those thinkers who at present, as in the past, confuse image with perception, by making a perception out of image (art as portrait, copy, or imitation of nature, or history of the individual and of the times, etc.), and, worse still, by making a sort of image out of perception which is to be grasped by means of the "senses." But perception is no more and no less than a complete *judgment* and as such signifies image and category—or system of mental categories which govern image (reality, quality, etc.). Moreover, with respect to image or *aesthetic a priori synthesis* of feeling and fancy (intuition), perception is a new synthesis, of representation and category, of subject and predicate: *logical a priori synthesis.*

As to the latter, it would be advisable to repeat everything that has been said regarding the former, and, above all, that in it content and form, representation and category, subject and predicate, do not exist as two elements joined together by a third element, but representation exists as category and category as representation in indivisible unity. For the subject is such only in relation to the predicate, and the predicate is such only in relation to the subject. Perception, then, is neither a logical activity among other logical activities, nor the most rudimentary and imperfect of them; but he who knows how to dig out all the treasures it contains has no need to search beyond it for other species of logicalness. For out of perception are born as twins (perception itself being this synthetic gemination) consciousness of what actually happens (which in its prominent literary forms assumes the name of *history*) and consciousness of the universal (which in its prominent forms assumes the name of system or *philosophy*). Philosophy and history, for no other reason than that of the synthetic nexus of the perceptual judgment from which they originate and in which they live, constitute the higher unity that philosophers have discovered with their identification of philosophy and history, and that men of common sense discover, in their own way, whenever they observe that ideas suspended in midair are phantoms, and that the only things true and worthy of being known are the events which occur, the real events. Furthermore, through perception (the variety of perceptions) it is possible to explain why the human intellect endeavors to go beyond them and to superimpose on them a world of types and laws governed by measurements and mathematical relations; that is to say, why, besides philosophy and history, *natural and mathematical sciences* are constructed.

It is not my task here to present an outline of Logic[d] as I have done and am doing in the case of Aesthetics. Therefore, setting aside the job of determining and expounding the nature of logic and of intellectual, perceptual, or historical knowledge, I will resume the line of argument, not proceeding this time, however, from the artistic and intuitive spirit, but from the logical and historical, which has transcended the intuitive by elaborating image into perception. Does the spirit find satisfaction in this form?

To be sure, everybody knows the very intense satisfactions of knowledge and science. Everybody through experience is acquainted with the burning desire that takes hold of us to unveil the face of reality, hidden by our illusions. And, no matter how terrible that face be, its discovery is never divorced from a profound sense of satisfaction: the satisfaction in the possession of the truth. But is this satisfaction, in contrast to the preceding one of art's, perhaps, complete and final? Along with the satisfaction of knowing reality, does not dissatisfaction appear on the scene too, maybe? Even this is most certain, and that dissatisfaction with knowledge (as everybody likewise knows through experience) manifests itself in the longing for action. To know the actual condition of things is all well and good, but our knowledge of it must be for the sake of action. Yes, let us know the world in the best possible manner, but in order to change it: *tempus cognoscendi, tempus destruendi, tempus renovandi.*[4]

No man stops at knowledge, not even the skeptics or pessimists, who, as a consequence of that knowledge, assume this or that attitude, adopt this or that way of life. And indeed, the retention of knowledge acquired, that "retaining" after "having understood," without which (to put it, as always, with Dante)[5] "no knowledge is produced," the construction of types, laws, and canons of measurement, the natural and mathematical sciences, to which I referred a short while ago, constitute a going beyond theoretical to practical activity. Not only does each one of us know from experience (verifiable as it is always by factual test) that such is really the case, but, if we give the matter some thought, it will be seen that it cannot be otherwise. It was believed at one time (and even at present by not a few unconscious Platonists, mystics, and ascetics) that knowing involved an uplifting of the soul to a God, an Idea, a world of ideas, an Absolute, existing above the phenomenal world of man. And it was natural that when the soul, alienated from her-

---

[4] ["A time to know, a time to destroy, a time to rebuild."]

[5] [Dante, *Divina Commedia, Il Paradiso,* V, 41–42. It should be noted that Croce changes Dante's verb "fa" (line 41) to its reflexive form, "si fa," for reasons of grammar.]

self by an effort contrary to nature, had reached that higher sphere, she returned to earth stupefied. She could have been per-petually blessed and at leisure there, only that thought about knowing, which was no longer a thought, had as its counterpart a reality which was not reality.

But, ever since knowledge came down to earth (with such authors as Vico, Kant, Hegel, and similar archheretics) and has come to be conceived not as a more or less faded copy of an unchanging reality, but as a continual human effort producing not abstract ideas but concrete concepts (syllogisms and his-torical judgments, perceptions of reality), action has no longer been something which represents a degradation of knowledge, another expulsion from heaven to earth or from paradise to hell, nor has it been even something which we are in a position to accept or reject at will, but something which entails theory itself, being a requirement of it. And as goes the theory, so goes the action. Our thought is historical thought about an his-torical world, process of development about a development; and no sooner has the attribute of a reality been articulated than the attribute no longer holds because it has itself produced a new reality which awaits a new attribute. A new reality, which comprises the economic and moral life, transforms intellectual man into practical man—the man of politics, the saint, the man of industry, the hero—and elaborates the *logical a priori synthesis* into *practical a priori synthesis*.[e] But this new reality is, somehow, always a new feeling, a new desiring, a new willing, a new passionateness, in which not even the spirit can rest, in-asmuch as it solicits first of all, as new material, a new intuition, a new lyric, a new art.

Thus, the last term of the series (as I had stated at the begin-ning) becomes reunited with its first. The circle is closed again, and the cycle begins anew. This cycle is a recurrence of the cycle already completed, whence the Vichian concept of "recurrence," to express it with the word made classic by Vico himself.[f] Still, the development I have sketched explains the independence of art, as well as why it has seemed dependent to those who enter-tained the erroneous doctrines (hedonistic, moralistic, conceptualistic, etc.) which I criticized in the foregoing, though not without pointing out in criticizing them that each of them was alluding to some truth. If it is asked which of the various activities is real or if they are all real, we must reply that none is real because what is real is only the action of all those activities —an action which does not rest on any of them in particular. Of the various syntheses that we have distinguished in succession—aesthetic synthesis, logical synthesis, practical synthesis— the sole real one is the *synthesis of syntheses*: the Spirit, which is the true Absolute, the *actus purus*. However, in another respect, and for the same reason, all of them are real within the unity of the spirit, within the eternal cycle and recurrence which constitutes their eternal constancy and reality.

Those who used to see or continue to see art in terms of concept, history, mathematics, type, morality, pleasure, and every other thing are right because there are within it (by virtue of the unity of the spirit) these and all the other things. In fact, this existence of all of them, together with the persistent onesidedness of art (as well as of any other particular form) which tends at the same time to reduce them to one alone, explains the passage from one form to the other, the fulfillment of one form in the other, and development. Still, those very persons are also wrong (in virtue of the aspect of distinction, which is inseparable from unity) because of the manner in which they reveal the aforesaid things: all abstractly on a par, or in confusion. For concept, type, number, measurement, utility, pleasure, and pain, exist in art *qua* art, as either antecedents or consequents—or to be more exact—as both antecedents and consequents; and for this reason, they exist there either as presuppositions (set aside and forgotten, to make use of a favorite expression from De Sanctis), or as premonitions. Without that element of presupposition, without that element of premonition, art would not be art; but it would not be art either (and all the other forms of the spirit would be confused thereby), if our intention were to impose those prerequisites on art as such—which is, and can never be anything but, intuition. The artist is always unblamable morally and uncensurable philosophically, even though his art may have for subject matter an inferior morality and philosophy. Insofar as he is artist, he is not a man of action and does not reason, but poetizes, paints, sings; in short, he expresses himself.

Were another criterion adopted, one could then proceed to condemn Homeric poetry as did the Italian critics of the seventeenth century and the French critics at the time of Louis XIV who turned up their noses at what they called the "mores" of quarreling, chattering, uncouth, cruel, and ignorant heroes.[g] Criticism could well be made of the philosophy underlying Dante's poem, but that criticism will only penetrate, as through a tunnel, the subsoil of Dantesque art, and will leave intact the surface itself, which is after all its art. Niccolò Machiavelli[h] may uproot Dante's political ideal by no longer recommending as reliable liberator a supranational emperor or pope, but a tyrant or a national prince; yet he will not have uprooted the Dantesque lyric in behalf of that aspiration. Similarly, it could be recommended that certain paintings, novels, dramas be not shown to, nor be read by, children and the youth. However, this recommendation and act of prohibition will involve the practical side of things and will not affect the works of art themselves, but rather the books and canvases which serve as instruments for the reproduction of art, and which, insofar as tangible works, not only get priced in the market at a value convertible into gold or grain, but likewise lend themselves to being shut up in a study or closet, and even to being burned in a "pyre of vanities" à la Savonarola.[i]

To confuse, out of a mistaken yen for unity, the various phases of development, to pretend that morals governs art at the moment when, on the contrary, the latter transcends the former, or that art governs science at the moment when the latter governs or transcends art, or has itself for quite some time been governed and transcended by life—here is what unity well understood (which is at the same time rigorous distinction) should reject and avoid. It should also reject and avoid it because the systematic determination of the various phases of the circle makes it possible to understand not only the independence and the dependence of the various forms of the spirit, but the *normal preservation* of some in the others as well. Of the problems which present themselves in this connection, it is convenient for me to mention one of them, or better still, to go back to it again since I have already alluded to it, namely, the relation between fancy and logic, between art and science.

This problem, after all, is essentially the same as that which reappears as the investigation of the distinction between *poetry* and *prose*, ever since at least (and the discovery was reached early, being already found in Aristotle's *Poetics*) it has been recognized that the distinction is not to be carried through with the criterion of nonmetrical or metrical writing, inasmuch as we can have poetry in prose (for example, novels and dramas) and prose in verse (for example, didactic and philosophical poems). It may be carried through, of course, with a more rigorous criterion—such as the one we have made clear—of image and perception, of intuition and judgment, where poetry is the expression of image, and prose the expression of judgment or concept. But actually, the two expressions as such are of the same nature, and both of them have the same aesthetic value. For if the poet is the lyricist of his feelings, so the prose writer is likewise of his, that is, a poet, even as regards the feelings born to him out of and within conceptual investigation. Now, there is no reason to recognize the poetic quality in a composer of a sonnet and deny it to those who have composed the *Metaphysics,* the *Summa Theologica,* the *Scienza Nuova,* the *Phaenomenologie des Geistes,*[j] or have told the story of the Peloponnesian War, the politics of Augustus[k] and Tiberius,[l] or have given an account of "universal history," since in all of these works there is as much passion and as much lyrical and representative quality as in any sonnet or poem. Thus, all the distinctions that have attempted to restrict the poetic quality to the poet and to deny it to the prose writer are like those stones carried with great effort to the top of a steep mountain, only to come tumbling down into the valley again.

To be sure, one may readily anticipate a difference. However, in order to determine it, it is vain to separate poetry and prose in the manner of naturalistic logic, as two coordinate concepts simply at odds with each other; rather, it is necessary to conceive them developmentally, as a passage from poetry to prose. And, in connection with this passage, just as the poet by virtue of the unity of the spirit not only presupposes an emotional material, but retains his state of passion by raising it to the poetic level (the passion for art), so the thinker or the prose writer not only retains that same state by raising it to a passion for science, but in addition retains the intuitive quality. Whence his judgments emerge expressing simultaneously the emotional state bound up with them, and so retain their artistic character along with their new scientific one. We can always contemplate this artistic character by presupposing its scientific counterpart, that is to say, by ignoring and taking no interest in science criticism itself in order to enjoy the aesthetic form which it has assumed. This explains also why science belongs equally, though under different aspects, to the history of science and to that of litera-ture, and why amidst the various types of poetry enumerated by rhetoricians it is, to say the least, capricious to refuse to in-clude "the poetry of prose" which is at times much more genuine poetry than so much pretentious poetry of poetry. Incidentally, it would be well for me to refer again to another problem of the same order to which I have also alluded in passing: the prob-lem of the relation between art and morals. Though the imme-diate identification of one with the other has been denied, their relationship must now be reaffirmed, noting that, just as the poet frees himself from every other passion but keeps his passion for art, so at the same time he retains through the latter a sense of duty (duty toward art). Thus, every poet during the act of creating is moral because he fulfills a sacred function.

The order or the logic of the various forms of the spirit, rendering them mutually necessary and therefore all necessary, exposes the error of denying one in favor of the other: the error of the philosopher (Plato), the moralist (Savonarola or Proudhon[m]), the naturalist and the practical man (there are too many to bother with their names!), all of whom reject art and poetry. Conversely, it also exposes the error of the artist who reacts against criticism, science, the practical, morals, as did so many "romantics" in tragedy and as so many "decadent" authors repeat at present in comedy. These are errors and follies which can also be somewhat overlooked (in keeping always with our objective not to leave anyone completely unhappy) because it is evident that through their negative attitude itself they make a positive contribution of their own, namely, as revolt against certain false concepts or certain false manifestations of art and science, of practical and moral life (for example, Plato's criticism of the notion of poetry as "wisdom," Savonarola's criticism of the lax and, hence, decadent and rapidly disintegrating culture of the Italian Renaissance, etc.). However, it would be utterly foolish to think that philosophy would lack something without art, on the ground that what conditions its problems would be missing, and that to make it prevail alone against art would be depriving it of the very air it breathes; that practical life is not such unless it is moved and inspired by aspirations and, as they say, by "ideals," by "precious imagination," which is after all art. And conversely, it would be equally foolish to think that art without morality—the art which, according to decadent authors, usurps the title of "pure beauty" and before which incense is burned as in a festival of a diabolical idol—as a result of the defective moral life in which it is born and which surrounds it, destroys itself as art and becomes caprice, luxury, and charlatanry, with the artist no longer serving it (art), but it serving, like the vilest of slaves, his private and futile interests.

Even so, against the idea of the circle in general, which is so helpful in making intelligible the independence relations between art and the other forms of the spirit, has been raised the objection that this idea exhibits the work of the spirit as an annoying and melancholy doing and undoing, a monotonous going around in circles which is not worth the bother.[n] Of course, there is no metaphor that does not offer some room for parody or caricature—which, however, after having amused us for a while, obliges us to return seriously to the thought which is expressed in the metaphor itself. Now, thought is not a sterile repetition of a cycle that recurs, but rather, as is evident, a continual enrichment of a cycle that recurs and keeps recurring. The last term, which becomes first again, is not the old first, but manifests itself as a manifold and precise set of concepts, as an experience of a fuller life, including even the experience of works contemplated—which the originally first term lacked— thus offering material for a more lofty, more refined, more complex, more mature art. Accordingly, instead of an ever-monotonous spinning, our notion of the circle is then nothing but the true philosophical idea of *progress*, of the perpetual growth of the spirit and of reality itself, where nothing except the form of growth is repeated. Unless we wish to object to a man who walks, that his walking is a standing still because he always moves his legs with the same rhythm!

Another objection, or rather another sign of rebellion, against the same idea may be frequently noted, though it may not be too articulate. It is the feeling of restlessness existing in some or in a few, their desire being to destroy and transcend the circularity which is the principle of life in order to arrive at a region where it is possible to rest from the anxieties of life, and where one may look behind at the threatening wave by standing on the shore away from the ocean. But I have already had occasion to say what this desire for refuge is. Beneath all the appearance of exaltation and sublimation, it is actually denial of reality— which one doubtless may experience, but it is called death: the death of the individual, but not that of reality, which does not die nor does it fret over its coming and going, but enjoys it. And others dream of a higher form of the spirit in which the circle is resolved—a form which is supposed to be Thought of Thought, unity of the Theoretical and the Practical, Love, God, or some such name. Yet they do not realize that this thought, this unity, this Love, this God already exists within the circle and throughout the circle, and that these but duplicate uselessly an investigation already completed or repeat the already known in metaphorical fashion, almost as in the myth of another world which re-enacts the drama itself of the one and only world.

The drama which I have up to now outlined is really ideal and extratemporal in nature, and I have made use of the terms first and last for semantic convenience alone in order to designate the logical order. It is ideal and extratemporal because there is no moment or individual in which it is not fully revealed, as there is no particle of the universe which is not animated by the spirit of God. But the ideal aspects, indivisible within the ideal drama, may be seen as separate things in empirical reality, as bodily symbols of ideal distinctions. Not that these aspects are really separate (ideality is true reality), but appear empirically that way to those who view them as types, since there is no other way to figure out from types the individuality of facts, to which they turn their attention, except by expanding and exaggerating the ideal distinctions. Thus, it seems that the artist, the philosopher, the historian, the natural scientist, the mathematician, the man of affairs, the good man live independently of each other— these distinctions constituting the spheres of artistic, philosophical, historical, scientific, mathematical culture, and of economic and moral life, with all the institutions that are connected with them. So it also appears that even the life of mankind throughout the centuries is divided into ages in which one or the other or just a few of the ideal forms get represented: ages of poetic fancy, of religion, of speculation, of science, of industry, of political passions, of moral enthusiasms, of the worship of pleasure and so forth—and these ages have their more or less complete cycles and recurrences. However, amidst the uniformity of individuals, of classes, of ages, the person who possesses the eye of the historian discerns perpetual differences; and the one who possesses the mind of the philosopher, discerns unity in difference; and the historian-philosopher sees in that difference and unity ideal progress as historical progress.

But let us also speak for a moment as empiricists (inasmuch as empiricism, if there be such a thing, is of some benefit) and ask ourselves which type is our age entering or which one is it leaving, or what is its dominant character. To this question the unanimous answer will be: that our age is, or has been, scientific in culture, industrial in practice; and also, with one accord, that both philosophical and artistic greatness will be denied to it. But, since (and here is where empiricism really gets into trouble) no age can live without philosophy and without art, similarly, even our own age has had the one as well as the other, to the degree that it could have had them. Its philosophy and its art— the latter immediately, the former mediately—appear before thought as documents of what our age has really been, in its complexity and entirety, by interpreting which documents we may render clear to ourselves the situation from which our *duty* ought to stem.

Contemporary art is sensual, has an insatiable appetite for pleasure, is replete with restless urgings toward an ill-understood aristocracy manifesting itself as an ideal of voluptuousness, or of violence and cruelty. At times, it longs for a mysticism which is likewise egoistic and voluptuous—with no faith in God and none in reason, incredulous and pessimistic, and often most effective in expressing such states of mind. This art, which the moralists condemn in vain, upon being afterward understood in its profound motives and in its genesis, calls for action which will surely not be inclined to condemn, to repress, or to rectify art itself, but to direct life more vigorously toward a healthier and deeper morality, which shall beget a nobler art in content and, I would like to add, a nobler philosophy. A nobler art than that of our own age, which is incapable of giving an account not only of religion, science, and itself, but even of art as such, which has become an unfathomable mystery or, rather, a subject of horrible absurdities among positivists, neo-criticists,° psychologists, and pragmatists, who until now have been almost the only representatives of contemporary philosophy, and who have relapsed (doubtless, in order to reacquire new powers and to think out new problems!) into the most childish and crudest concepts of art.

IV. *Criticism and the History of Art*

Literary and art criticism is often conceived by artists as a harsh and tyrannical *pedagogue*, who gives capricious orders, imposes prohibitions, permits liberties, and thus does good or harm to their works by determining their fate at his pleasure. And for this reason artists either become submissive, humble, flattering, adulatory before criticism, while abhorring it in their hearts; or, on the other hand, when they do not achieve their purpose or their fiery spirit prevents them from stooping to those tricks of the flatterer, they rebel against it by denying its usefulness, by cursing it, by ridiculing it, and by comparing the critic (to recall my own case) to an ass entering a potter's shop and crushing to pieces with its *quadrupedante ungulae sonitu*[1] the delicate art products left drying in the sun.

The fault this time, to tell the truth, lies with the artists, who do not know what criticism is, inasmuch as they expect favors from it which it is not in a position to grant and fear penalties which it is not in a position to inflict. For it is clear that just as no critic can make an artist out of a person who is not one, so no critic could ever, owing to its metaphysical impossibility, destroy, ruin, or harm even to a slight degree an artist who is an artist. These things have never happened in the course of history, they do not occur in our day, and we may rest assured that they will never happen in the future. However, on other occasions, it is the critics themselves, or the self-styled ones, who actually assume the role of pedagogues, oracles, art guides, legislators, seers, and prophets. They dictate to the artists that they do this and not that. They assign them themes, and declare certain subjects as poetic and others as not. They are dissatisfied with the art being produced at present, preferring something akin to the art which used to be produced in this or that age of

[1] ["Kicking hoofs."]

the past, or another kind which they say they foresee in the near or distant future. They reproach Tasso for not being Ariosto, Leopardi for not being Metastasio,[a] Manzoni for not being Alfieri, D'Annunzio for not being Berchet[b] or Fra Iacopone.[c] They draw a sketch of the great artist of the future, providing him with ethics, philosophy, history, language, metrics, coloristic and architectonic techniques, and with everything else which in their opinion, he needs.

It is clear this particular time that the fault lies with the critic. Before such ferocious animals, the artists are right in behaving, as one does with animals which we try to tame, fool, and frustrate, by placing them at our service or by getting rid of them or by sending them to the slaughterhouse when they are no longer good for anything. To the credit of criticism, however, it is necessary to add that those capricious critics are not so much critics as they are artists—unsuccessful artists, who tend to aspire to a certain form of art unattainable by them, either because the tendency itself was contradictory and vacuous, or because they lacked ability. And thus, they harbor within their hearts the bitter feeling of an unfulfilled ideal; they cannot speak of anything else but that ideal, lamenting its absence everywhere and advocating its presence everywhere. Moreover, sometimes, they are anything but unsuccessful artists—indeed, quite successful —but the very force of their personality makes them incapable of understanding objectively other forms of art different from their own, and for this reason they are prone to reject them outright.

What contributes to such rejection is the *odium figulinum*,[2] the jealousy of the artist toward his fellow artist, the envy, which is doubtless a defect, but a defect of which many excellent artists are so guilty that we should not deny them the same indulgence we apply to the faults of women, given the fact that they are so inseparable from their amiable qualities. The other artists should calmly reply to these critic-artists: Continue doing what you do so well with your own art, but allow us to do what we can with our own. And their reply to the unsuccessful artists

2 ["Professional hatred."]

and unqualified critics should be: Do not expect us to do what you did not know how to do yourselves, or know what the work of the future is going to be, about which neither of us knows anything! As a matter of fact, this is not the usual answer because passion gets in the way. But that is really the logical answer, and with that answer the question is logically settled, even though one must anticipate that the dispute will not come to an end, but will last as long as there are both intolerant and unsuccessful artists, in other words, forever.

There is another conception of criticism, which is represented by the magistrate and the *judge,* as the preceding one is by the pedagogue and the tyrant. It assigns to criticism not the task indeed of promoting and guiding the life of art—which is promoted and guided, if one wishes to call it so, by history alone, that is, by the total movement of the spirit in its historical course —but rather, the task of simply discriminating the beautiful from the ugly in the art which has already been produced, by sanctioning the beautiful and censuring the ugly, with all the solemnity characteristic of stern and conscientious sentences.

But I fear that not even with this new definition can the stigma of uselessness be removed from criticism, although perhaps the motive behind the same stigma may change somewhat. Is there really a need for criticism to discriminate the beautiful from the ugly? The production itself of art is never anything else but this discrimination since the artist attains purity of expression precisely by eliminating the ugly which threatens to invade it. This ugliness represents his human passions which rebel against the pure passion of art, such as his weaknesses, his prejudices, his comforts, indifference, haste, having one eye on art and the other on the spectator, the publisher, the impresario. All these things interfere with the artist's physiological gestation and with the normal birth of his expression of image, with the poet's melodious and creative verse, with the painter's precision at drawing and his blending of colors, with the composer's melody. So much so that, if they are not careful about guarding themselves against such things, they introduce into their works sonorous but empty verses, inaccuracies, dissonances, discords.

Now, just as the artist is a judge during the period of production (and a very severe judge of himself, whom nothing escapes
—not even what escapes others), so the latter themselves, by
virtue of the spontaneous character of contemplation, likewise
immediately and very effectively discern where the artist has
been artist and where he has been human, all too human; also,
in which works or in which parts of the works reign supreme the
lyrical spirit and creative fancy, or where these have become
congealed and have succumbed to other things which pretend
to be art—hence are called "ugly" (when viewed from the standpoint of this pretension). Of what use, then, is the verdict of
criticism, especially since it has already been pronounced by
genius and taste, which are legion, are everyman's, and are matters of general and age-old consent? So much is this the case that
the verdicts of criticism always arrive either too late to sanction
forms already formally sanctioned by universal applause (one
must not confuse, however, genuine applause with hand clap-
ping and with worldly clamor, nor the steadiness of glory with
the fickleness of fortune), or they arrive too late to condemn
uglinesses already condemned, disliked, forgotten, or even
praised by mouth for that matter, though in bad faith, owing to
partiality and obstinate pride.

Criticism conceived as magistrate kills the dead or breathes
on the face of what is very much alive anyway, imagining as it
does that its very breath is the breath of God, the restorer of life!
Accordingly, it performs a useless task—useless because it has
already been taken care of beforehand. I would like to ask
whether critics have been responsible for establishing the greatness of Dante, Shakespeare, or Michelangelo, or, on the contrary, the great number of their readers and spectators. Still, let
me ask whether to these latter who have applauded and continue to applaud those greats there cannot be added, as is quite
natural, literary men and professional critics too, since their
applause does not differ in this respect from that of all the
others, and even from that of children and the general public—
all of whom are equally ready to open their hearts to the beautiful which speaks to everyone, except that sometimes it does not

do so out of spitefulness, when it detects the stern look of a critic acting as judge.

Thus, there arises a third conception of criticism: criticism as *interpretation* or *commentary*, the function of which is to humble itself before works of art and restrict itself to clarifying a picture, by placing it in its proper setting, furnishing data about the period in which it was painted and what it represents; to explaining the linguistic forms, historical references, and the factual and theoretical presuppositions of a poem. In either case, once its task has been accomplished, it permits art to work spontaneously in the spectator's and reader's mind, which will then judge according to what his personal taste dictates. The critic, in this instance, is conceived as a cultured guide or a patient and discreet schoolteacher. "Criticism," as a famous critic[d] has indeed defined it, "is the art of teaching how to read."[3] Echoes of this definition may still be heard.

Now then, no one would question the usefulness of guides in museums and at exhibits, of reading teachers, and much less of learned guides and scholars, who know so many things hidden from most people and who are able to shed much light. Not only does the art farthest from us in time need these aids, but the art of the immediate past called contemporary, which, although it treats of subjects or assumes forms that seem obvious, is not always sufficiently so. At times, a considerable effort is needed to train people to feel the beauty of a short poem or any work of art, even if it was only born yesterday. Prejudices and habits and forgetfulness interfere with access to the work, and it requires the expert hand of the interpreter or the commentator to eradicate or rectify them. Criticism in this sense is undoubtedly most useful, but, after all, we do not understand why it should be called criticism, especially since that sort of work has its appropriate name, to wit, interpretation, commentary, exegesis. At the least, it would be better not to call it such, so as not to provoke an annoying misunderstanding. Misunderstand-

[3] [Charles A. Sainte-Beuve, *Portraits littéraires,* III, new ed. (Paris: Garnier, n.d.), 546. In the Italian rendition of the passage in French, Croce changes Sainte-Beuve's definition of the "critic" to fit "criticism."]

ing, because criticism is eager to be, wants to be, and is, something else. Its function is not to invade art, nor to rediscover the beauty of the beautiful and the ugliness of the ugly, nor to lower itself before art, but rather to raise itself to the level of great art and, in a certain sense, go beyond it.[4] What, then, is genuine and true criticism?

First of all, criticism is a *combination of all the three* things which I have hitherto analyzed, that is to say, all three of them are its necessary condition, without which it could not arise. Without the factor of art (as we have seen, art versus art is, in a certain sense, that view of criticism which claims to be productive or an aid to production or censor of certain forms of production for the benefit of others), criticism would lack the material with which to work. Without taste (criticism as judge), the critic would lack the experience of art—the art assimilated by his spirit, separated from nonart and enjoyed apart from the latter. And finally, this experience would not exist without exegesis, that is, without the elimination of obstacles to reproductive fancy, furnishing as it does the spirit with those presuppositions of historical knowledge which the latter needs, and which constitute the kindlings burning in the fire of fancy.

But before going any further, it would be wise to settle a serious doubt which has appeared and is apt to reappear frequently as much within the field of philosophical literature as within popular thought, and which certainly, were it justified, would not only affect adversely the possibility of criticism of which we have been speaking, but also that of the reproductive fancy itself or taste. Is it really possible, after all, to collect, as exegesis purports to do, the materials needed for reproducing another's work of art (or our own past work itself, searching our

---

[4] "It is a happy moment for the critic as well as for the poet when either one or the other can each, in his own fashion, cry out with that ancient [Archimedes]: *Eureka!* The poet discovers the region where his genius can henceforth live and grow; the critic discovers the instinctive basis and the ruling principle of that genius." (Sainte-Beuve, *Portraits littéraires*, I, 31). [Croce's footnote, the only one in the text, quotes from the original, which is in French. Incidentally, this footnote did not appear in the first edition (1913) of the *Breviario*.]

memory and consulting our notes in order to recall in what state we were when we produced it), and to reproduce in fancy that work of art in its genuine features? Can the collection of materials ever be complete? And, however complete it may be, will fancy ever permit itself to be chained thereto in its work of reproduction? Or will it not operate as a new product of fancy by introducing new material? And will it not be obliged to do so anyway, owing to its actual inability to reproduce the work of others and of the past? Is the reproduction of the individual, of the *individuum ineffabile,* conceivable, especially since every sound philosophy teaches that the universal alone is eternally reproducible? Consequently, is not the reproduction of works of art of others or of the past perhaps a pure impossibility? Besides, is not what is usually taken as an accepted fact in ordinary conversation and as the implicit or explicit presupposition of every dispute over art perhaps but *une fable convenue* (as was said of history in general)?

In truth, to speculate on the problem somewhat extrinsically, it seems highly improbable that the firm faith (shared by everyone) in the comprehension and understanding of art should lack foundation, especially when one considers that those very persons who, theorizing abstractly, deny the possibility of reproduction, or, as they say, the absoluteness of taste, are indeed extremely stubborn in clinging to their own judgments of taste.[e] For they know quite well the difference between the assertion that I like or do not like wine because it agrees or disagrees with my physiological make-up, and the assertion that one poem is beautiful, and another ugly. The second type of judgment (as Kant showed in a classic analysis) carries with it the incoercible claim to universal validity. So much so that people get excited over such judgments, and, in days of knighthood, there were even those who defended, sword in hand, the beauty of the *Gerusalemme,* whereas, to our knowledge no one has let himself be killed for asserting his like or dislike of wine! Moreover, it would not be valid to object that the most artistically shameful works of art are liked too by many or by someone, and if not by others, by their authors at least. For what is being questioned here is not whether they are liked (since nothing can arise in the mind without its consent and, hence, without a corresponding pleasure), but whether that pleasure is an aesthetic pleasure, and whether it is based upon a judgment of taste and beauty.

Passing from an extrinsic to an intrinsic consideration of the problem, it is pertinent to state that the objection against the conceivability of aesthetic reproduction rests upon a reality conceived in turn either as a clash of the atoms or as abstractly monadistic, composed of monads without intercommunication and harmonized only from without. But reality is no such thing. Reality is spiritual unity, and nothing there is lost, everything being eternally present. Not only the reproduction of art, but, in general, the recollection of any event (which is, after all, always reproduction of intuitions) would be inconceivable without the unity of the real. And if we were not ourselves Caesar and Pompey,[f] that is, that universe which was once determined as Caesar and Pompey and is now determined as something living within us, we could not form any idea of Caesar and Pompey. Furthermore, the doctrine that individuality is irreproducible and that the universal alone is reproducible doubtless belongs to "sound" philosophy, but to sound scholastic philosophy, which separated the universal and individual, made the latter the accident of the former (the dust swept away by time), and ignored that the true universal is the universal individualized, and that the only true *effabile* is the so-called *ineffabile*, the concrete and individual.

And, finally, what does it matter if we do not always have available the material to reproduce with complete exactness all the works of art or a single work of art of the past? The complete reproduction of the past is, as every human work, an ideal, which is realized *ad infinitum*, and, for this very reason, is always realized according to what is permitted by the structure of reality at each moment of time. Is there not in a poem a nuance whose full significance escapes us? No one will want to claim that that nuance, of which we now have a dim vision that does not satisfy us, will not manage to become more precise in the future, as a result of studies, reflection, and the rise of favorable conditions and congenial circumstances. Therefore, the more taste is confident of the legitimacy of its stand, the more historical investigation and interpretation are untiring in restoring and preserving and increasing the knowledge of the past. Let the relativists and the skeptics of taste and of history go as far as to utter, from time to time, their desperate cries, which do not persuade anyone, not even themselves, as we have seen, of the effectiveness of their despair over our power to judge.

Nevertheless, now that we have finished with the long but indispensable parenthesis, let us take up again the thread of the argument. Though art, historical exegesis, and taste constitute *antecedents* of criticism, they do not constitute *criticism* itself as yet. In fact, with that triple presupposition, we achieve nothing but the reproduction and enjoyment of the image expressed; that is to say, we go back and place ourselves more or less in the situation of the artist-producer re-enacting the production of his image. Nor can we escape from that situation with a proposal, as some boast, to reproduce in a new form the work of the poet and of the artist by offering an equivalent: wherefore they define the critic as *artifex additus artifici*.[5] For that reproduction in new dress would be a translation, or a variation, another work of art, inspired in some way by the first; on the other hand, if it were the same, it would be a reproduction pure and simple, a material reproduction, with the same words, the same colors, the same tones, in short, useless.

The critic is not *artifex additus artifici* but *philosophus additus artifici*.[6] His task is not realized until the image acquired is preserved and transcended at the same time. It pertains to thought, which we have seen surpass and shed new light on fancy, render intuition as perception, define reality, and, therefore, distinguish reality from unreality. From this perception, from this distinction (which is always essentially criticism or judgment), art criticism, with which we are now dealing in particular, is born asking whether and to what extent the ma-

[5] ["Artist added to artist."]
[6] ["Philosopher added to artist."]

terial, which is on hand as a problem, is *intuition,* that is, real as such, and whether and to what extent it is not so, that is, unreal—reality and unreality being in art called beauty and ugliness, corresponding to truth and error in logic, profit and loss in economics, good and evil in ethics. Thus, all art criticism may be reduced to the following very brief proposition, which nonetheless is sufficient to differentiate its work from that of art and of taste (which considered in themselves are logically mute), and from expository erudition (which lacks logical synthesis and, hence, is itself also logically mute): "There is a work of art *a*"—or its corresponding negative—"There is not a work of art *a.*"

This proposition sounds trivial, but no more so than did the definition of art as intuition, which on the contrary was afterward seen to include so many things, so many affirmations and negations—so very many that, even though I have proceeded and continue to proceed analytically, I have been unable and shall be unable to offer but a few pointers. To begin with, the proposition or judgment of art criticism—"There is a work of art *a*"—implies first of all, as every judgment, a subject (the intuition of the work of art *a*), to arrive at which requires the effort of exegesis and creative reproduction, together with the discriminating power of taste. As we have seen, this is often a difficult and complicated matter, where many go astray through lack of creative ability or through deficiency and superficiality of culture. In addition, it implies, as every judgment does, a predicate, a category, and in this instance the category of art, which must be embodied in the judgment, thereby becoming the concept of art.

Moreover, we have also seen how many difficulties and complications arise from the concept of art and how it is always difficult of attainment, being as it is continually assaulted and plotted against, hence, needing to defend itself against such assaults and plots. Art criticism, for this reason, develops and grows, falls and rises, with the development and fall and rise of the philosophy of art. Thus, each one of us may compare what art criticism was in the Middle Ages (when it can almost be said not to have existed) and what it became in the first half of the nineteenth century with Herder[g] and Hegel and the romantics, and in Italy with De Sanctis[h]; and in a narrower sense, what it was with De Sanctis, and what it became in the subsequent naturalistic period when the concept of art went into eclipse, going so far as to be confused with physics and physiology and even with pathology. And, if half or less than half of the disagreements on judgments of art are based upon lack of understanding as to what the artist has done, upon lack of sympathy and taste, the other half or more than half stem from the insufficient clarity of the ideas on art. Whence it often happens that two individuals are substantially in agreement with respect to the value of a work of art, except that one approves vocally what the other disapproves, because each one of them refers to a different definition of art.

Because of this dependency of criticism on the concept of art, there are as many forms of false criticism to distinguish as there are of false philosophy of art. To limit ourselves to the chief forms of which we have already spoken, there is a criticism that, instead of reproducing and characterizing art, fragmentizes and classifies it. There is another, the moralistic, which treats works of art as actions related to goals which the artist had in mind or should have had in mind. There is the hedonistic, which approaches art as something that has or has not achieved sensuousness and diversion. There is the intellectualistic, which measures the advancements of art against the advancements of philosophy. In Dante, it recognizes his philosophy but not his passion; it judges Ariosto weak because it finds in him a weak philosophy, Tasso more serious because he has a more serious one, and Leopardi contradictory in his pessimism. There is criticism which separates content from form—usually called psychological—and which, instead of paying attention to the works of art, pays attention to the psychology of the artists as men. There is another one which abstracts forms from content and is delighted with abstract forms because, depending on individual cases and sympathies, they remind it of antiquity or of the Middle Ages. There is still another which finds beauty wherever there are rhetorical embellishments. And finally, there is the one which, having determined the laws of genres and of the arts, accepts or rejects works of art according to whether or not they approximate the models constructed.

I have neither enumerated all the varieties of criticism, nor did I intend to do so, nor would I even want to expound the critique of criticism, since it would be nothing more than a repetition of the criticism and dialectic of the Aesthetics sketched above. Besides, the beginnings of the unavoidable repetition should have been evident from the few pointers already given. More profitable would it be to summarize (except that even a brief summary might require too much space) the history of criticism, and affix historical names to the ideal positions I have pointed out. This would show how the criticism based on models became the rage especially in French and Italian classicism, conceptualistic criticism in German philosophy of the nineteenth century, moralistic criticism in the period of religious reform or of the Italian *Risorgimento,* and psychological criticism in France with Sainte-Beuve and so many others. Furthermore, it would show how hedonistic criticism is popular particularly with judgments of men of the world, of salon and journalistic critics, while criticism based on classifications is popular in schools, where it seems that the function of criticism is conscientiously fulfilled when we have investigated the so-called origins of meters, "technique," "themes," literary and artistic "genres," and when we have enumerated the representatives included under the various genres.

Still, the forms which I have described in summary fashion are, however erroneous, forms of criticism. This cannot be truthfully said of other forms which raise their banners and fight among each other, one assuming the name of "aesthetic criticism" and the other that of "historical criticism," and which I request permission to baptize instead, as they deserve, *pseudo-aesthetic criticism* (or aesthetistic criticism) and *pseudohistorical criticism* (or historicistic criticism). These two forms, despite their intense antagonism toward each other, share a hatred of philosophy in general and of the concept of art in particular.

They are against the use of thought in art criticism, which, according to the former, falls within the competency of artistic souls, and, according to the latter, within that of the erudite. In other words, both underrate criticism as such, the former reducing it to pure taste and enjoyment of art, the latter to pure expository investigation or the collection of materials for creative reproduction.

What aesthetics, which implies thought and concept of art, has to do with pure taste without concept is hard to say. And what history has to do with unorganized erudition on art—which is unorganizable as history because it lacks the concept of art and is ignorant of its nature (in contrast, history always requires knowledge of its subject matter) is even harder to ascertain. And the most we could ever do is to keep taking note of the reasons for the peculiar "fortune" these terms have undergone. Aside from this, there would be nothing wrong with those names nor with their refusal to practice criticism, provided that the exponents of either trend would really stay within the limits set by themselves, where one group would enjoy works of art and the other would gather materials for interpretation; and provided that they would allow those who want to do criticism to do it, or would rest content with speaking ill of criticism as long as they do not tackle the problems appropriate to it.

To acquire this attitude of abstention, it would be necessary more or less that aesthetes not open their mouths, but go into ecstasy about art and ruminate its joys in silence; and, at best, on meeting their own kind, that they understand each other, as it is said that animals do, without speaking—who knows, after all, if this be not true! Thus, their faces spontaneously expressive of rapture, their outstretched arms expressive of wonder, or their hands joined together in a prayer of thanksgiving for the joy experienced: these should tell the whole story. The historicists, for their part, could of course speak—speak of codices, corrections, chronological and topical data, political events, biographical incidents, sources of the work, idiom, syntax, meters, but never of art. They are at art's service, but as pure men of learning they cannot raise their eyes to gaze at its face, just as the manservant does not raise his eyes to look his mistress in the face, yet he brushes her clothes and prepares her food: *sic vos, non vobis.*[7]

But just try to request of men, however outlandish they be in their ideas and fanatic about their absurdities, such abstentions and sacrifices and heroic deeds! In particular, try to ask the person who for one reason or another has dabbled in art all his life not to speak of it and not to judge it! Just as the speechless aesthetes talk and judge and reason about art, so likewise do the inconclusive historicists. And, since with respect to the subject in question they lack the guide (despised and abhorred by them) of philosophy and of the *concept* of art—and they certainly need a concept—when common sense by chance does not suggest to them unconsciously the one which is correct, they roam amidst all the miscellaneous *preconceptions*—moralistic and hedonistic, intellectualistic and content-istic, formalistic and rhetorical, physiological and academical—which I have mentioned, now choosing one and now choosing another, now mixing them all up together and contaminating them. And the most curious spectacle (though foreseeable by the philosopher) is that in their nonsensical talk about art, the aestheticists and the historicists (irreconcilable enemies starting from opposite points) agree with each other so well that they end up uttering the same absurdities. Nothing is more amusing than to recognize the stalest intellectualistic and moralistic ideas in the pages of impassioned lovers of art—so impassioned that they hate thought—and in the pages of the most positivistic historians, so positivist that they are afraid of compromising their own position if they attempt to understand the object of their investigations, which happens to be called art this time!

True art criticism is doubtless *aesthetic* criticism, not because it scorns (as pseudoaesthetic criticism does) philosophy, but rather because it operates as philosophy, and from a conception of art. Moreover, it is *historical* criticism not because, like its pseudohistorical variety, it sticks to what is extrinsic to art, but rather because, after once having availed itself of historical data

7 ["Thus you (work), but not for yourself" (Virgil).]

for creative reproduction (so far it is not history as yet) and having ascertained that there is creative reproduction, it *becomes history* only when the nature of that event it has reproduced in the fancy is determined, that is, when the event is described thanks to the concept and when the event which has really taken place is established. Thus, with respect to the positions inadequate to criticism, the two tendencies that are at odds coincide in criticism—[so-called] *historical art criticism* and [so-called] *aesthetic criticism* being the same thing. It makes no difference which term we employ, since each one may be of particular use only for reasons of timeliness, as when we wish, for example, as regards the former to call attention more pointedly to the necessity of understanding art, and as regards the latter, to the historical objectivity of the treatment. So in like manner, the problem posited by certain methodologists as to whether history forms part of art criticism as means or as end becomes resolved. For it is now clear that that history which is used as means, precisely because it is means, is not history, but expository material; and that history which is of value as end, is certainly history, except that it does not form part of criticism as a particular element but, rather, constitutes the whole thing—which is what the word "end" expresses exactly.

However, if art criticism is historical criticism, it follows that the task of discerning the beautiful and the ugly cannot limit itself simply to approving and disapproving, as occurs in the immediate consciousness of the artist insofar as he creates or of the man of taste insofar as he appreciates. Its task should be amplified and raised to the level of what is called *explanation.* And since in the world of history (which is, of course, *the* world) negative or privative events do not exist, what appears to the taste to be repugnant and ugly for not being artistic, when considered historically, will be neither repugnant nor ugly. For history is aware that what is not artistic may well be *something else,* and has its own right to be—a right so legitimate as to have existed.

The powerful Catholic allegory which Torquato Tasso wrote for the *Gerusalemme* is not something artistic. Neither are the patriotic harangues of Niccolini[i] and Guerrazzi,[j] nor the subtleties and conceits which Petrarch introduced in his lofty, graceful, and melancholic verses. But Tasso's allegory is one of the manifestations of the Catholic Counter-Reformation in Latin countries; Niccolini's and Guerrazzi's harangues constitute drastic attempts to incite the minds of Italians against the foreigner and the priest, or to win adherents to this method of revolt; Petrarch's subtleties and conceits represent a devotion to traditional troubadour elegance, revived and enriched in the new Italian civilization—that is, they are all practical matters, worthy of respect and historically quite significant. Of course, for linguistic vividness and in keeping with current parlance, we could continue to speak, in the field of historical criticism, of the beautiful and of the ugly, provided that we make manifest at the same time, or allude and let it be understood, or at least not exclude, the *positive* content not only of the *beautiful* but of the *ugly,* which after all could never be so unconditionally condemned in its ugliness as when it is *fully justified and understood,* because only then is it removed in the most unconditional way from the sphere of art.

For this reason, art criticism, when it is truly aesthetic or historical, through its very process develops into *criticism of life,* since it is not possible to judge, that is to say, to determine the peculiar characteristic of works of art, without at the same time judging the works of all life, assigning to each its own character. This is seen in truly great critics, and above all in De Sanctis, who is as profound a critic of art as he is of philosophy, ethics, and politics in his *Storia della letteratura italiana* and in *Saggi critici*—so profound in the one because profound in the others, and vice versa—the strength of his pure aesthetic treatment of art constituting the strength of his pure moral treatment of morals, of his pure logical treatment of philosophizing, and so on. For the forms of the spirit of which criticism avails itself as categories of judgment are, to be sure, ideally distinguishable within unity, but not materially separable from each other and from unity, unless we wish to see them suddenly wither and die. The usual distinction of art criticism from other forms of criticism, therefore, simply serves to indicate that the attention of the speaker or the writer is addressed to one aspect rather than another of the sole and indivisible subject matter.

Empirical likewise is the distinction, which I have retained until now in my terminology for purposes of didactic clarity, between *criticism* and *history* of art. This distinction arises principally from the fact that in the investigation of contemporary literature and of art there is dominant the judging or polemical accent (for which the word "criticism" seems to be more fitting), while in the investigation of more remote literature and art, the narrative accent is dominant, and so is called more appropriately "history." Actually, true and successful *criticism* is the dispassionate *historical narration of what has happened.* History is the only genuine criticism that can be applied to human events, which cannot be nonevents since they have happened, and which are not controllable by the spirit in any other manner except by *understanding them.* And as art criticism has appeared to us inseparable from other varieties of criticism, so also it is solely for reasons of literary emphasis that the history of art could ever be separated from the general history of human civilization, within which it doubtless follows its own law—that of art—but from which it receives the historical impetus belonging to the spirit as a whole and never to one of its forms, severed from the others.

Appendix Notes

NOTE a, p. 4. Michel E. de Montaigne (1539–1592), French essayist and moralist, born in Périgord, famous for his *Essays,* first published in 1580.

NOTE b, p. 6. For this obvious allusion to Plato (427–347 B.C.), see Benedetto Croce, *Aesthetic as Science of Expression and General Linguistic,* 2nd ed., trans. Douglas Ainslie (London: Macmillan, 1922), pp. 158–159.

NOTE c, p. 8. *Ibid.,* Part I for Theory of Aesthetics (1–152), Part II for History of Aesthetics (155–474).

NOTE d, p. 9. Gustav Theodor Fechner (1801–1887), German physicist and philosopher, born in Gross Sarchen (Lower Lusatia), exponent of experimental aesthetics. For Croce on Fechner in aesthetics, *ibid.,* pp. 394–397.

NOTE e, p. 14. Armida is the sorceress, "the Circe of the Christian Era," in *Jerusalem Delivered* (Italian original, 1593) by Torquato Tasso (1544–1595), Italian poet of the Counter-Reformation in Italy, born in Sorrento.

NOTE f, p. 14. Giuseppe Parini (1729–1799), Italian poet and priest, born in Bosisio, author of *Il Giorno* (1763–1801), a satire on the Italian nobility of his day.

NOTE g, p. 14. Vittorio Alfieri (1749–1803), Italian poet, born at Asti, in Piedmont.

NOTE h, p. 14. Alessandro Manzoni (1785–1873), Italian novelist, born in Milan, author of *I promessi sposi* (English trans., *The Betrothed*).

NOTE i, p. 14. Giuseppe Mazzini (1805–1872), Italian patriot and statesman, born in Genoa, leader of the struggle for the unification of Italy during the *Risorgimento* and advocate of the republican movement throughout Europe.

NOTE j, p. 16. Gottfried Wilhelm Leibniz (1646–1716), German philosopher and mathematician, born in Leipzig, discoverer of calculus. For Croce on Leibniz in aesthetics, *Aesthetic,* pp. 207–209.

NOTE k, p. 17. Friedrich W. J. von Schelling (1775–1854), German philosopher, born in Leonberg, author of *The System of Transcendental Idealism* (German original, 1800). For Croce on Schelling, *Aesthetic,* pp. 291–295.

NOTE l, p. 17. For Croce on Hegel, *ibid.,* pp. 297–303.

NOTE m, p. 17. Hippolyte Taine (1828–1893), French literary critic and historian, born in Vouziers. For Croce on Taine, *ibid.,* pp. 392–394.

NOTE n, p. 17. The Herbartians were members of the school of Johann Friedrich Herbart (1776–1841), German philosopher, born in Oldenburg, anti-Hegelian. For Croce on Herbart, *ibid.,* pp. 307–311.

NOTE o, p. 19. For Croce on Aristotle (384–322 B.C.), *ibid.,* pp. 169–170; on the seventeenth-century "ferments" in aesthetics, pp. 189–203; on Vico, pp. 220–234.

NOTE p, p. 19. For Croce on Baumgarten, *ibid.,* pp. 212–219.

NOTE q, p. 19. For Croce on Kant, *ibid.,* pp. 272–282; on the Leibnizians and Wolffians, disciples of Johann Christian Wolff (1679–1754), German philosopher and mathematician, born in Breslau, himself disciple of Leibniz and systematizer of the rationalist tradition in Germany, pp. 210–212.

NOTE r, p. 19. For the conception of artistic "form" in De Sanctis, see *Saggio critico sul Petrarca* (Naples, 1869).

NOTE s, p. 23. Friedrich Theodor Vischer (1807–1887), German aesthetician, born in Ludwigsburg, Hegelian in aesthetics, described by Croce as "the bulkiest of all German aestheticians, indeed the German aesthetician *par excellence,*" *Aesthetic,* p. 336.

NOTE t, p. 25. Francesco Petrarca (1304–1374), Italian poet and humanist.

NOTE u, p. 25. Lodovico Ariosto (1474–1533), Italian poet, born in Reggio, author of *Orlando Furioso* (1516).

NOTE v, p. 25. Ugo Foscolo (1778–1827), Italian patriot, poet and writer, born on the Ionian Isle of Zante, author of *I Sepolcri* (1807).

NOTE w, p. 25. Giacomo Leopardi (1798–1837), Italian poet and moralist, born in Recanati.

NOTE x, p. 25. Gabriele D'Annunzio (1863–1983), Italian poet, novelist, and publicist, born in Pescara.

NOTE y, p. 26. Walter Pater (1839–1894), English essayist, born in London.

NOTE z, p. 27. Henri-Frédéric Amiel (1821–1881), Swiss poet and literary critic, born in Geneva, of French descent.

LECTURE TWO

NOTE a, p. 28. For the polemic in aesthetics between the formalists (Herbartians) and the content-ists (Hegelians), *Aesthetic*, pp. 311–313, 370–387.

NOTE b, p. 30. Eduard von Hartmann (1842-1906), German philosopher and aesthetician, born in Berlin. For Croce on Hartmann, *ibid.*, pp. 378–381, 448–449, 454–455.

NOTE c, p. 30. This "human interest" concept of aesthetic content is a reference to the theory of Karl Koestlin, German aesthetician and author of *Aesthetik* (1869). For Croce on Koestlin, *Primi saggi,* pp. 32–34; also, cf. *Aesthetic,* pp. 376–377.

NOTE d, p. 32. For more on Croce's critique of this distinction, *ibid.*, pp. 111–117.

NOTE e, p. 34. Phidias (*ca.* 500–*ca.* 432 B.C.), Greek sculptor, born in Athens.

NOTE f, p. 34. Apelles, Greek painter who flourished in the latter part of the 4th century B.C.

NOTE g, p. 37. For Croce on natural and artistic beauty, cf. *ibid.*, pp. 98–100, 104–110, 339–349, 459–460.

NOTE h, p. 38. For the history of the doctrine of Rhetoric, *ibid.*, pp. 422–436.

NOTE i, p. 39. The apt analogy here comes from Zeno of Citium (flourished *ca.* 300 B.C.), founder of the Stoic School; see *ibid.*, p. 189.

NOTE j, p. 40. A description of Vico's; cf. *ibid.*, p. 226.

NOTE k, p. 40. *Estetica come scienza dell'espressione e linguistica generale* (Milan: Sandron, 1902). For Croce's demonstration of this identity, *Aesthetic,* pp. 140–152.

Note l, p. 41. Cf. *ibid.,* pp. 436–458, for Croce's historical account of the theory of the artistic genres and of the theory of the various arts.

Note m, p. 43. Gotthold Ephraim Lessing (1729–1781), German critic and dramatist, born in Saxony, author of *Laocoön* (original, 1766). For Croce on Lessing, *Aesthetic,* pp. 266–268, 449–452.

Note n, p. 46. Guido Cavalcanti (*ca.* 1250–1300), Italian poet and friend of Dante (1265–1321).

Note o, p. 46. Cecco Angiolieri (*ca.* 1260–*ca.* 1312), Italian poet, born in Siena.

Note p, p. 46. Merlino Cocaio, pseudonym for Teofilo Folengo (1496–1544), Italian poet, born in Mantua, author known for his burlesque ("macaronic") verses.

Note q, p. 46. Annibale Caro (1507–1566), Italian author, translator, and poet, born in Ancona.

Note r, p. 46. Pietro Sarpi (1552–1623), Italian historian and theologian, born in Venice, anti-Jesuit.

Note s, p. 46. Daniello Bartoli (1608–1685), Jesuit historian and theologian, born in Ferrara, rector of the Jesuit College in Rome.

LECTURE THREE

Note a, p. 52. For Foscolo's correspondence with Countess Antonietta Fagnani Arese, see Vol. I of his *Epistolario,* ed. Plinio Carli, *Edizione nazionale delle opere di Ugo Foscolo,* XIV (Florence: Felice Le Monnier, 1949), 209–414.

Note b, p. 53. The translator has searched for this quote, but to no avail.

Note c, p. 53. It should be borne in mind that "perception" in Croce means *conception,* that is, knowledge by concepts, in contradistinction to "intuition," which is knowledge by direct acquaintance.

Note d, p. 54. For Croce's theory of logic as "the science of pure concept" (Vol. II of his system), consult the Selected Bibliography on the subject.

NOTE e, p. 56. For Croce's practical philosophy (Vol. III), consult the Selected Bibliography.

NOTE f, p. 56. For Croce's cyclical theory of history (Vol. IV), consult the Selected Bibliography.

NOTE g, p. 58. Cf. *Aesthetic,* pp. 33, 183.

NOTE h, p. 58. Niccolò Machiavelli (1469–1527), Italian political author, born in Florence, best known as the author of *The Prince* (1532). Croce's reference here reflects the great clash in medieval Italy between the Guelphs, who opposed the German imperial rule in Italy, and the Ghibellines, who defended it.

NOTE i, p. 58. Girolamo Savonarola (1452–1498), Italian preacher and reformer, born in Ferrara, joined the Dominican order, was accused of heresy, strangled, and burned to death.

NOTE j, p. 59. Aristotle is, of course, the author of the first work cited, St. Thomas Aquinas (1225–1274) of the second, Vico of the third, and Hegel of the fourth and last.

NOTE k, p. 59. Augustus, Julius Caesar (63 B.C.–A.D. 14), first emperor of Rome.

NOTE l, p. 59. Tiberius, Claudius Caesar (42 B.C.–A.D. 37), second emperor of Rome.

NOTE m, p. 60. Pierre Joseph Proudhon (1809–1865), French socialist, born in Besançon. For Croce on Proudhon's moralistic approach to art, *Aesthetic,* p. 399.

NOTE n, p. 61. Croce's most formidable critic of his conception of the spirit as a "circle" was Giovanni Gentile, who accused it of being like a "mad dog" running after its own tail!

NOTE o, p. 64. Successors of a school of thought inspired in Kant, whose philosophy is technically known as "criticism."

LECTURE FOUR

NOTE a, p. 66. Metastasio, Greek form of the surname of Pietro Trapassi (1698–1782), Italian poet, born in Rome, author of opera libretti.

NOTE b, p. 66. Giovanni Berchet (1783–1851), Italian novelist and poet, born in Milan.

NOTE c, p. 66. Fra Iacopone (*ca.* 1230–1306), Italian poet from Todi, Franciscan mystic.

NOTE d, p. 69. Charles-Augustin Sainte-Beuve (1804–1869), French literary critic and historian, born in Boulogne-sur-Mer.

NOTE e, p. 71. For Croce's approach to this question of aesthetic absolutism versus aesthetic relativism, cf. *Aesthetic,* pp. 122–124, 466–470.

NOTE f, p. 72. Pompey (106–48 B.C.), Roman general and statesman.

NOTE g, p. 75. Johann Gottfried Herder (1744–1803), German writer, philosopher, literary critic, theologian, born in Mohrungen (East Prussia). For Croce on Herder, *ibid.,* pp. 250–256, 339–340, 434–435, 452, 461.

NOTE h, p. 75. For De Sanctis as a literary critic, see his classic two-volume work, *Storia della letteratura italiana* (1871); English edition, *History of Italian Literature,* trans. Joan Redfern (New York: Harcourt, Brace, 1931).

NOTE i, p. 80. Giovanni Battista Niccolini (1782–1861), Italian writer and poet, born in Bagni di San Giuliano (Lucca), liberal and anticlerical in political thought.

NOTE j, p. 80. Francesco Domenico Guerrazzi (1804–1873), Italian patriot, statesman and writer, born in Leghorn.